PROGRAMS FOR YOUTH

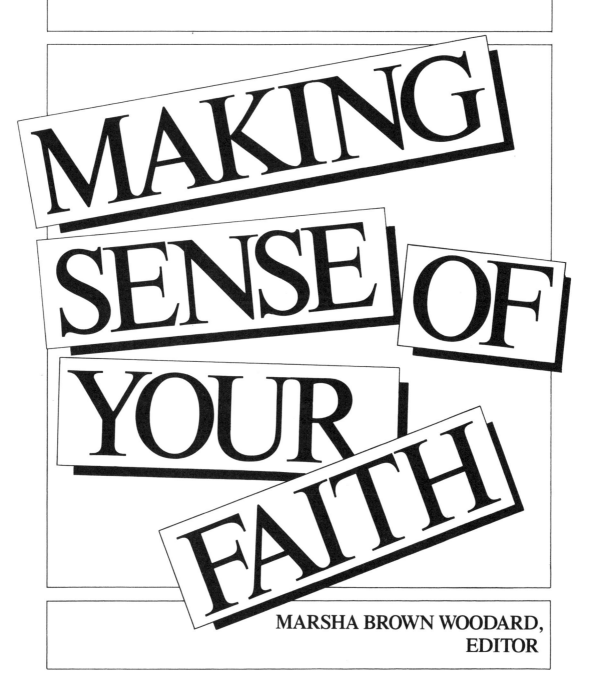

MAKING SENSE OF YOUR FAITH

MARSHA BROWN WOODARD,
EDITOR

Judson Press ® Valley Forge

Unless otherwise indicated, Bible quotations in this volume are from the Revised Standard Version of the Bible, copyrighted 1946, 1952 ©, 1971, 1973 by the Division of Christian Education of the National Council of the Churches of Christ in the U.S.A., and used by permission.

Other quotations of the Bible are from

Good News Bible, the Bible in Today's English Version. Copyright © American Bible Society, 1976. Used by permission.

The New English Bible, (NEB). Copyright © The Delegates of the Oxford University Press and The Syndics of the Cambridge University Press, 1961, 1970.

HOLY BIBLE New International Version, copyright © 1978, New York International Bible Society. Used by permission.

Library of Congress Cataloging-in-Publication Data

Making sense of your faith.

  1. Youth—religious life. I. Woodward,
Marsha Brown.
BV4531.2.M35 1987   268'.433   87-3367
ISBNO-8170-1122-6

Writers

Rev. Jay W. Flair
Jay is a graduate of the University of North Carolina and Duke Divinity School. He currently serves on the staff of Koinonia Partners, Americus, Georgia, and previously served as associate pastor of Northwestern Baptist Church in Southfield, Michigan. He is married and has a son.

Rev. Donald Harrington
Don is a graduate of Franklin College in Franklin, Indiana, Colgate Rochester Divinity School, and Graduate Theological Union. Don is currently pastor of First Baptist Church in Sturgis, Michigan. He brings years of experience in Christian Education as well as other aspects of ministry. He is married and has a son and a daughter.

Rev. Soozi Whitten Ford
Soozi is a member of the faculty of Sterling College in Sterling, Kansas, where she is currently serving as Assistant Professor of Christian Education. She has worked with youth on the local, regional, and national levels. She is married and has one daughter.

Mrs. Elizabeth J. Loughhead
Bettie is a graduate of Colgate Rochester Divinity School. She served as director of Religion and Community Life at Colorado Women's College. She is currently administrator of Elder Care, an adult day care center at Calvary Baptist Church, Denver, Colorado. She is married and has two sons and a daughter.

Rev. Marsha B. Woodard
Marsha is a graduate of Ottawa University, Ottawa, Kansas, and Eden Theological Seminary, Webster Groves, Missouri. She served as Minister of Christian Education at Antioch Baptist Church, St. Louis, Missouri, and is currently serving as Program Associate in the Department of Ministry With Youth.

Rev. Marcia Patton
Marcia has served in American Baptist churches in New Jersey, Utah and Pennsylvania and is currently working on a doctorate in Psychoeducational Processes at Temple University in Philadelphia, Pennsylvania. Marcia has a long involvement in youth ministry through staff positions, conference leadership, teaching, and writing.

Rev. Jeffrey D. Jones
Jeff is a graduate of Brown University, Andover Newton Theological School and Villanova University. He was past director of the Department of Ministry With Youth and is currently serving as interim pastor at First Baptist Church in Pitman, New Jersey. He is married and has two sons.

Rev. Clara E. Wong
Clara is a graduate of Mount Holyoke College and Colgate Rochester Divinity School. She has worked with junior and senior high youth in a variety of settings. She is currently the pastor of the Community Baptist Church in Allenville, Wisconsin.

Rev. Steve Youd
Steve is a graduate of Gordon College and Yale Divinity School. He formerly served as state director of youth and young adult ministries for the American Baptist Churches in Massachusetts. Currently he is serving as pastor of Covenant Baptist Church in Sandwich, Massachusetts. He is married and has three daughters.

Rev. Alonza Lawrence
Alonza is a graduate of Virginia Union and Virginia Union School of Theology. He is the pastor of Westwood Baptist Church, Richmond, Virginia. Alonza has worked in youth ministry for over ten years and as a teacher in the Richmond Public Schools for over six years. He is married and has a son.

Contents

Introduction

Words, words, words. Daily we are bombarded with words. Many faith words are tossed about—used but never explained. For youth this often leads to a partial or limited understanding of words important to our faith. In this volume, *Making Sense of Your Faith*, a number of writers have taken words important to the Christian faith and developed sessions that will help increase youths' understanding. These sessions will be challenging to youth, leading them to discover more than dictionary definitions of the words by encouraging them to seek understanding in light of Scripture and history, as well as their own experience.

As editor I am excited by the approach taken by the authors in this volume. Writing from years of experience in working with youth, each author brings gifts of wisdom, insight, and practical experiences. Many of the sessions have already been used with youth groups by the authors. The authors encourage youth to look seriously at their commitment to be disciples of Jesus Christ and at what this commitment means in their daily living.

In writing this volume we have had a particular audience in mind. We have written for youth who are fourteen to eighteen years of age or who are in ninth to twelfth grades. These are probably youth who have made an initial faith commitment. An initial faith commitment for youth who are from the Baptist tradition would be a profession of faith and baptism; for youth from other faith traditions this would be confirmation. These youth have begun a process that will con-

tinue throughout their lives—the process of growing in their understanding of what it means to be followers of Christ. While we expect that youth of this age range will be our primary audience, we feel the resource can be used with younger youth or with older youth who have not yet made an initial faith commitment. Some suggestions are given in the "Adaptation and Explanation" column throughout the volume.

Persons growing in their understanding of discipleship continually make new faith commitments. Throughout this volume there will be opportunities for youth to make a variety of commitments. Since we realize that no two youths will be at the same place, we do not expect that all youth will be making the same commitments. In looking at the ministry of Jesus Christ, we learn that commitment was not the same for everyone. For some it meant leaving their jobs to follow Jesus; for others it meant making restitution to those they had defrauded; for others it involved learning to accept persons they had viewed as outsiders; for others it meant staying in their hometown but acting differently. For all it was a process of growing or becoming more than they had been.

Peter is an example of this growth process. Throughout the Gospels we see Peter making new commitments as his level of understanding increases. We can also assume that this happened with others. Indeed, it is our hope for the youth in our midst that they will continually seek to gain new understandings of what it means to be a faithful follower—and that these understandings will lead to new commitments. Our hope in providing a variety of options is that when the time is right each youth will be able to make commitments that will provide the greatest challenge for his or her growth. By allowing opportunities for prayer and rededication, as well as times to make verbal commitments, you can create a climate of choice and not coercion within your group. It might be possible for these commitments to be shared with your larger church family as an affirmation of the ways in which youth are taking their faith seriously.

Tips for Leaders

The specific role of the leader will vary for each youth group. In some settings the leader will be one who is responsible for the total youth ministry program in the church. Other settings will call for a leader who is responsible for a particular program or a segment of a program. In other settings there will be a leadership team responsible for planning and implementing programs. This volume lends itself to use in any of these settings.

Wherever possible, we encourage a model of shared leadership in the planning and implementing of these sessions. A team of adults and youth—including both male and female, clergy and laity—would be ideal. In this way a variety of gifts are shared with the groups and several styles of leadership are experienced. The shared leadership model makes concrete the concept that all people have gifts for ministry and that these gifts can be shared in a variety of ways. Sharing leadership often helps groups become sensitive to a wider perspective on issues and reminds the group that there can be more than one way to respond to many situations. Another strength of shared leadership is that it can provide opportunities for youth and adults to be in ministry together, to learn from each other, and to accept mutually the responsibilities of providing leadership to a group.

Whether they are adult or youth, leaders will need to be:

- familiar with the needs and interests of members of the group;
- willing to adapt sessions so that they focus clearly on interests or needs that persons are currently experiencing;
- familiar with the materials, willing to make arrangements and gather resources;
- able to use a variety of learning/teaching methods such as films, tapes, newsprint, discussion, etc.;
- willing to share their own faith journeys and commit themselves to growing as followers of Christ.

Sessions

Each session has been written to stand by itself, and it is possible to use the sessions in a variety of orders. For example, several sessions can be used together to provide a more in-depth look at a particular word. For a group wishing to use this resource as an elective course, the sessions, as presented, allow for building on previous sessions and having a sense of continuity.

Use in a Church School Setting

In a church school setting this resource could be used either as a primary source or a supplemental resource with another curriculum. If your church school period lasts only forty-five minutes, you might consider using one session for two periods. You might choose to use the session as a supplemental resource for a particular word that corresponds with your current curriculum focus.

Use in a Retreat Setting

The sessions in this book lend themselves to easy adaptation for a weekend retreat.

Friday evening	1 session
Saturday morning	2 sessions
Saturday afternoon	1 session and free time
Saturday evening	1 session
Sunday morning	1 session and closing worship

Words, Words, Words

Marsha B. Woodard

Explanation and Adaptation	Program
	Objective: • To encourage youth to identify words of faith that are important to their understanding of what it means to be a disciple. **Overview of the Session:** A. Getting Started B. We Use Words C. Looking at Words of Faith D. The Meaning Makes a Difference E. Closing **Resources and Materials Needed:** Tape recorder, radio, newsprint, markers, Bibles, dictionaries, concordance. **The Session in Detail:** A. *Getting Started* Decorate the meeting space with words. These might be pages from the newspaper or magazines, individual words written on sheets of paper, headlines, phrases from advertisements, and so on. The idea is to create an image of lots of words.
The idea here is to have words coming from more than one source. Have newsprint available and possibly two writers. Get as many words from the group as quickly as possible.	B. *We Use Words* After the group has gathered, have a tape recorder and a radio going. After a few minutes, turn them off. 1. Begin by saying, "Words are all around us. We see them, we hear them, we think them. We use them every day of our lives. Let's quickly brainstorm a list of all the words that are important to us or that we use frequently." 2. Now ask the group to make a second list, this time

Explanation and Adaptation	Program

	listing all the words that they can think of related to their faith or to being a Christian.
	
	3. Look at the second list and ask the group if they use these words as much as those on the first list. Why or why not?
	
	4. Ask the group to look again at the second list. Ask individuals to find three words they can define and three words they are not sure of and list these on a piece of paper. Have the group members walk around the room to see if they can find someone who can define one of the words they did not know and also to see if they can define a word for someone else.
	
	5. After a few minutes have the group gather again. Explain the following, saying something like this:
	
	    Many times words used to explain our faith are never fully explained. We may use them because we have heard them. Sometimes when we don't understand, we decide that the words are old-fashioned and refuse to use them. When a new word is introduced, we may just avoid it. But our challenge as Christians is to try to understand these words in light of Scripture, history, and our own experience.
	
	C. *Looking at Words of Faith*
	  1. For this step you will need Bibles and dictionaries. A concordance would also be helpful.
	
	    Pray Joy
	    Disciple Peace
	    Love Parable
	    Faith
	
	    Divide the group into pairs or triads and ask each small group to find a dictionary definition of each word and to find Scriptures that might lead them to an understanding of each word. An option might be to give each group one or two words to allow more time for researching Scriptures. Ask each group to put its findings on newsprint for sharing with the total group.
	
	  2. Ask the total group to gather and share their findings. After all have shared, note points of similarity as well as points of difference. If the total group worked on all words, have them choose new partners and write their own definitions for each word. If your group worked on different words, then it might be easier to have them return to the same small

Explanation and Adaptation	Program

groups and write definitions for the words worked on.

D. *The Meaning Makes a Difference*
   1. What difference does it make?
      After the new definitions have been shared, ask the group what difference these words make to our faith. Encourage the group to list things about each word that make the word significant to the Christian faith. For example:

      • *Pray*—Describes a way of communicating with God; available to everyone; can be done at anytime, in any place.
      • *Disciple*—Name for persons who followed Christ; describes Christians; says that we have a leader; implies that followers are learners.
      • *Love*—There are different types of love; can be hard to do; reminds us that we have a responsibility; reminds us that God loved us first.
      • *Faith*—Believe in something outside yourself; hope for change; work for a different future.
      • *Joy*—Being happy; even when you are unhappy, you can think of times when you were happy.
      • *Peace*—Nonviolent; something to work towards or for; happens between people and between nations.
      • *Parable*—Type of story; used to help people understand important truths.

      As the group members reflect on the work they have done in this session, they will be able to create a list that describes how these words help us in understanding our faith.

E. *Closing*
   Look again at the list made at the beginning of the session. Identify other words that the group might want to explore. Share ways that this might be done. For example, the steps done in this session could be done by an individual at home with any of the words. The group might choose to make assignments for a future meeting. Possibly some words are words used in this volume, and the group could choose to do those sessions. The group might also spend time over several sessions learning one new word while having another focus.

Closing Litany

Leader: Words, words, words. We are bombarded with words.

Explanation and Adaptation	Program
	Group: Thank you, God, for words.
	Leader: We use them even when we don't fully understand them.
	Group: Thank you, God, for words.
	Leader: Words can help us, challenge us, and bring us joy.
	Group: Thank you, God, for words.
	Leader: Words can be understood; when they are, they help us grow.
	Group: Thank you, God, for words.
	Leader: Words of faith help us to be the persons God is calling us to be.
	Group: Thank you, God, for words.
	Leader: Yes, our lives are filled with words; but each word has a purpose, each word has a use.
	Group: Thank you, God, for words.
	After the litany the group might join together for a time of shared prayers.

Images of God
Marcia Patton

Explanation and Adaptation	Program

Our images of God come from many sources—pictures and stories from our childhood, words we use for God, hymns and songs we sing, and personal and private experiences. In this session we want to identify these images and push the edges a bit to include more.	**Objectives:**
	• To create a list of ways we see and understand God.
	• To reflect specifically on the image of God that is revealed in Jesus Christ.
	
	Overview of the Session:
	A. Preparation—Our Story
	   1. Reflect over the past week for images.
	   2. Brainstorm a list of our images.
	B. Development—General Consideration of Our Story
	   1. Search the Bible to add to our list.
	   2. React to the whole list.
	C. The Story—God with Us
	D. Integration—Sharing Questions and Insights
	E. Closing

Sharing even our hints of the meaning can make it more understandable to us.	**Materials Needed:** Pencils and paper for everyone, several different translations of the Bible, newsprint and markers or chalkboard and chalk.
How we understand God makes a difference in how we respond to God.	**The Session in Detail:**
Often we forget what a difference our environment can make to learning. Can the participants in the group be comfortable in your setting? Is it a setting where it will be possible to meditate, discuss, and write?	A. *Preparation—Our Story* To prepare for today's work, prepare the room. If you have access to posters or pictures, find pictures that reflect some of the images of God expressed in the biblical passages as well as others that show how God might be revealed in nature. If this is not possible, clear the room in such a way as to help participants be open to whatever images may come to mind. Blinds should be drawn away from windows to allow the out-of-doors into the room. Make the seating arrangement as com-

Explanation and Adaptation	Program
	fortable and flexible as possible so people can talk with one another with ease, be comfortable when doing the fantasy, stand up easily when doing the Bible drill, and so on.
Beginnings are important—to get the things the participants need to say (the football scores, etc.) out of the way yet allow the time you need to deal with the material.	1. Reflect over the past week for images. After participants arrive begin with a settling exercise. This might be as simple as an opening prayer or one-word summation from each person that describes how they "are" at this meeting. Then invite the group on a "fantasy," a time to think. Ask them to relax, close their eyes if that would help, take ten deep breaths, and relax their hands, feet, jaws, neck muscles. Then ask them to remember the week just past and make a list in their heads about where they have seen God. Slowly list the typical experiences for your group over the past week—school, family events, times with friends, walks they may have taken, music they have listened to, pictures they have seen, and so on.
If you have not done a "fantasy exercise" before, talk it through to yourself a couple of times. Give the instructions very slowly and deliberately, speaking in an even, low voice.	
Younger groups may not be ready for this kind of exercise—you might ask straightforward questions such as "How have you experienced or seen God this week in school?" or "How have you experienced or seen God this week at home?" or "How have you experienced or seen God this week in church?" or "What kind of pictures come to mind when you think of God?" Or you might start with the Bible drill first and then ask the other questions.	2. Brainstorm a list of our images. At the end of the exercise, ask participants to list on the chalkboard or newsprint the different ways they remember seeing or experiencing God. If necessary, have two people write at the same time so the listing will go faster. After the list has been made, give each participant a moment to copy it on a sheet of paper for individual use later.
	B. *Development—General Consideration of Our Story* 1. Search the Bible to add to our list. Using the following verses, add to the list you have started by using what the Bible gives us as some of the attributes of God. You may do this by asking people before class to be prepared to read or by having an old-fashioned Bible drill. If possible have a variety of translations for participants to use. If the various passages just reaffirm some things you have already listed, then star them on your chalkboard or newsprint list.
If your group is large, you might want to divide them into teams and assign different verses to different teams.	
You might make a game of charades out of the list and have the attributes acted by participants.	One who laughs—Psalm 37:13 One who smells—Genesis 8:21 One who whistles—Isaiah 7:18 One who rejoices—Isaiah 62:5 One who loves and hates—Isaiah 61:8 One who grieves—Genesis 6:6 Mighty—Joshua 4:24; Psalm 24:8 Living God—Deuteronomy 32:40; Jeremiah

Explanation and Adaptation	Program
	10:10 Steadfast love—Psalm 33:5; Psalm 145:11-20 Lord of hosts/King—Psalm 84:3 Living water—Jeremiah 17:13 Life—Deuteronomy 30:20 One who knows us—Psalm 139:23 Not a man—1 Samuel 15:29 Father—Isaiah 63:16; Psalm 89:26 Creator—Genesis 1 and 2; Psalm 136:1-9 Mother eagle—Psalm 32:11-12 Light—1 John 1:5 Love—1 John 4:7-8
Another way to do this is to use different symbols or colors. Add to the list some ways you react to the descriptions.	Give members a chance to add to their personal lists any of the above they may need to add. 2. React to the whole list. As individuals, mark the list you have created with the following: Circle those that surprise you. Put a + by those that make you comfortable. Put a * by those that make you uncomfortable. Put a ! by those that you think may be open to debate. Put a ? by those that raise questions for you. Put a > by those you want to explore further. Put a < by those that frustrate you.
It might be helpful to have the symbols listed on newsprint so that everyone can see. There may be some people in the group who have some insights about another's questions. Allow insights to be shared, but also affirm the questioner and allow the questioner to wrestle with the question if he or she needs to.	On a separate piece of newsprint, list the images that raised questions for them. List the ones that are open for debate. C. *The Story—God with Us* Have the following verses read by different participants: Hebrews 1:3 John 1:14 John 12:45 John 14:4 2 Corinthians 4:4 Mark 10:10 In journals or on sheets of paper or in one-on-one conversations, have participants answer these questions: How does Jesus Christ embody the images of God we have listed? How doesn't he? What does having Jesus come to earth mean for our image of God? How is it helpful? List any questions this idea raises.

Explanation and Adaptation	**Program**
	D. *Integration—Sharing Questions and Insights* Share in the total group the questions the last exercise raises for group members. Share their insights. What does our image of God mean for our everyday lives? How does it affect the way we act in the world?
	E. *Closing* As a way of bringing together the discussion today, do two things: • List all the questions raised on a piece of newsprint and ask each participant to choose a question to research during the week. Briefly discuss how they might do the research. Meditation; interviewing the pastor, church leaders, friends, parents; checking church library resources such as commentaries or Bible dictionaries, are all possibilities. • Have individuals or the group together reflect on these questions: What does it mean to believe in Christ as God incarnate (God with us)? How does it affect the way we live?
You may want to end with a circle of silence, letting each participant share his or her own questions and prayers with God in the silence. You may want to continue working on this theme with your group by using the next session in this book, "We Are Images of God."	To close the session you can have a litany around your questions—such as reading a question and then responding as a group with "Thank you, God, for our questions and our faith." Or you may want to read the list of attributes one by one, responding after each, "Thank you, God, for your presence among us."

We Are Images of God
Marcia Patton

Explanation and Adaptation	Program

Explanation and Adaptation

Groups with many younger youth may have some difficulty with this session. I would focus upon making the mirror, helping each individual find positive things to place in the mirror. You may choose to hear each person's story of his or her mirror after reading the Scripture, or you may lead a discussion that covers the following points:

1. When God created us, God declared us good and that goodness is not lost because of Jesus Christ.
2. God loves us as we are.
3. We are vehicles for God here and now to one another.

You might begin the discussion by asking, "What do you think about this statement?" and then reading one of the previous ones. Or you might have group members react to the statements on paper, writing their responses. Most important is that they see themselves as people God loves.

Program

Objectives:
- To write a personal understanding of *imago Dei*.
- To react with one another in terms of how we are the image of God for one another.

Overview of the Session:
- A. Preparation
- B. Our Story—Beginning
  1. What we like about our friends
  2. A look at ourselves—making a mirror
- C. Development—Our Vision
- D. The Story—Created in the Image of God
- E. Integrating Our Vision and the Story
  1. A better understanding
  2. How we see God in ourselves and one another
- F. Closing

Materials Needed:
Mirrors, newsprint and markers or chalkboard and chalk, paper and crayons or markers for each participant, Bibles for the readers.

The Session in Detail:

A. *Preparation*
   To ready the room, find as many mirrors as possible—full-length ones, hanging ones, hand-held mirrors, and so forth, and place them around the room. The more you have, the better. If possible, it would be good to have at least one mirror per participant, but it will not change the lesson plan if you cannot. If you can have more than one per participant, people could have a chance to choose.

Explanation and Adaptation	Program

You may want to make up several blank sheets—one with just a "mirror" drawn (to demonstrate how to use the whole paper), another with the "mirror" and the frame, another with the mirror divided into four sections. It is good to give the directions one step at a time, especially for younger groups.

A word, phrase, or picture that describes you

What your family name means or What your family means to you	Title of favorite song, book, music
Something that describes your future or your hopes	Something that describes your faith

---

You might want to give some illustrations of how this sharing and feedback might go. If your group is particularly encouraging of one another, you may instruct them to help to accentuate one anothers' positive points.

B. *Our Story—Beginning*

1. What we like about our friends
Greet each participant as he or she arrives. Ask how they have been since you were last together. Allow the usual flow of conversation. When you are ready to start in earnest with the lesson, ask the participants to think for a moment about their best friends. Have participants list things that they like about their friends, the attributes that make their friends, friends. List these attributes on newsprint or chalkboard.

2. A look at ourselves—making a mirror
Hand each of the participants a blank sheet of paper and a pencil, markers, or crayons. Tell them that they are going to make personal "mirrors." These "mirrors" will tell something about them in symbolic ways.

As they begin, ask the participants to choose a shape for their mirror. You might point to the ones in the room or suggest others that you have seen—oval, round, rectangular, square. Strongly suggest that they use up *most* of the sheet of paper that they have been given; pocket mirrors are not what we are talking about! Have them make a simple frame for the mirror and in the frame write a word or phrase that generally describes themselves.

Next have them divide the mirror into four equal sections. In one section have them put a word, phrase, or picture that describes either what their family name means to them or what they understand their family to be. In the second section have them put the title of their favorite song, music, or book—something that they feel best describes them. In the next section have them put a symbol, word, or phrase that describes their future or their hopes. In the last section have them put a symbol, word, or phrase that describes their religion or faith.

C. *Development—Our Vision*
After everyone has finished a mirror, have group members put them on the walls or on the mirrors around the room. Then have the participants circulate and look at each one. Next have the participants pair up with someone with whom they are comfortable and share

Explanation and Adaptation	Program
How does who we are affect how we act? *Imago Dei* means in the image of God. According to this passage, we have been made in the image of God. This is a major theological issue but one that may be internalized at this stage of our faith journey. It has important implications when it is applied to how we behave with one another. One possible discussion point is that being the image of God for others can be both positive and negative. How can this understanding help us to understand God? How can it hinder our understanding of God? The discussion might also include what being created in the image of God means about our responsibility to others. Another way to do the session: After the mirrors are made and the Scripture read, put each participant in the circle and have all the other participants say something positive about the person in the middle. Do this with each participant, then have a circle prayer, thanking God for each person in the group by name. You might want to develop an additional session if your group shows interest in more reflection on this topic. Combining the many images	the details of why they chose what they listed for each section of the mirror. The partners should feel free to ask for any clarification they may need or give any positive feedback they feel the person may have missed. D. *The Story—Created in the Image of God* Have the participants sit down together and read the creation story in Genesis 1:1-27 (or have it read by a group member who is a particularly good reader). Have the last two verses reread by two or three other readers, both male and female. E. *Integrating Our Vision and the Story* 　1. A better understanding 　Have the participants share with their partners how the "mirrors" they have made reflect something of how they are the "image of God." You might demonstrate this with a mirror you have done before the session with a friend of yours or with a person from the group whom you had as a partner. Encourage the participants to consider carefully what being made in the image of God means to them. You may want to give everyone a couple of minutes of directed silence before you ask them to share out loud with their partners. 　2. How we see God in ourselves and one another 　As people made in God's image, how do we come across as friends, as God to one another? This is something that the partners may want to share with each other or that the group may want to discuss as a whole. Keep the discussion focused in a positive light, understanding that part of the image of God is love. If questions arise that you or the group are not ready to deal with, record them on newsprint to be discussed in another session. F. *Closing* As you close this session, ask the participants to form a circle and pray for the partner they had during the session, remembering the partner's hopes and praying for his or her family and any concerns that may have come from the time of sharing.

Explanation and Adaptation	Program
of God with the many human images might help the group have a new understanding of the gifts and diversity in the human family.	

The Kingdom of God

J. W. Flair

Explanation and Adaptation	Program

Explanation and Adaptation

Altogether, the three Synoptic Gospels contain about 114 references to the "kingdom of God" (Matthew often uses the term "kingdom of heaven," which has the same meaning). This fact alone shows the importance of the kingdom in Jesus' ministry. That the kingdom was the central focus of Jesus' teaching and therefore of central importance to the Christian should be highlighted during the session.

For additional study related to the kingdom of God, see: *The Interpreter's One-Volume Commentary on the Bible*, edited by Charles M. Laymon (Nashville: Abingdon Press, 1982) pp. 1176–1186; *Sermon on the Mount*, by Clarence Jordan (Valley Forge: Judson Press, 1970); *A Theology for the Social Gospel*, by Walter Rauschenbusch (Nashville: Abingdon Press, 1978).

The founding dates of countries are usually listed in the dictionary.

Have the questions written on either newsprint or the chalkboard. Be sure and explain to the participants

Program

Objective:
- To help participants gain an understanding of the Christian concept of the kingdom of God and the central role it plays in their lives as Christians.

Overview of the Session:
- A. Getting Started
- B. The Shape of the Kingdom
- C. Parable Writing
- D. Citizens of the Kingdom
- E. The Value of the Kingdom
- F. Kingdom Mural
- G. Closing

Materials Needed:
Bibles, globe or world map, pencils, paper, dictionaries, newsprint, markers, large roll of paper, paint, crayons.

The Session in Detail:

A. *Getting Started*
Place a world map on the wall or a globe in the middle of the room. Attach to some of the countries a piece of paper that has the date the country was founded. As persons enter the room, hand them a pencil and piece of paper and have them study the map or globe for a minute. Then ask each one to write brief answers to the questions that follow. (Point out that these questions are about what they think or believe and are not intended to be a Bible fact quiz.)
- Where is the kingdom of God located?
- What is the date of the founding of the kingdom of God?

Explanation and Adaptation	Program
that these questions are simply to draw out what their personal thoughts and beliefs are regarding the kingdom; this is not a Bible quiz with right or wrong answers. If some persons finish earlier than others, you might suggest that they discuss their answers quietly with one other person. If you are short on time or people, choose fewer forms of government to define. Ask participants to develop a defense for the form of government they defined. The position that they defend may or may not be the form of government they would personally prefer. Keep in mind that the object of this exercise is to get participants to think about who rules the kingdom and what our individual roles in the kingdom are, and to compare and contrast God's kingdom with our earthly "kingdoms." The word "kingdom" could be translated "kingship" (from the Aramaic and the Greek) and speaks to an order that is different from those of our societal or governmental structures. We can learn a great deal about God's rule from Jesus' parables, but it is important to remember that much about the kingdom remains a mystery. In writing these parables, keep in mind these words from *The Interpreter's One-Volume Commentary on the Bible:* "A parable may be defined as an extended metaphor in which the comparison is based on a brief narrative rather than on a simple likeness to another object [as opposed to an allegory] . . . in which each element of a narrative repre-	• What does the kingdom of God look like? • Have you ever felt the presence of the kingdom? When all have finished writing, have those who are willing share their answers with the group. Have them read the following Scripture verses and discuss what they say in regard to the present and the future time and place of God's kingdom. Luke 17:20-21 Mark 1:14-15 Matthew 6:10; 12:28 Luke 11:2; 21:31 B. *The Shape of the Kingdom* Divide the participants into seven groups and have each group look up the dictionary definition of one of the forms of government listed below. Anarchy Communism Democracy Dictatorship Monarchy Socialism Theocracy Now give them some time to formulate an argument as to why that form of government should be used for the kingdom of God. Next, let each group present its case for its form of government to the entire group. After all the small groups have finished their presentations, have the total group decide which government, *if any,* would be best suited to the kingdom and why. C. *Parable Writing* Listed below are some of the parables that Jesus told about the kingdom of God. Divide the participants into groups of two or three persons and assign each group one of the parables. Then ask each group to write an original parable that makes the same point as the one Jesus told. An easy way to do this is to write a "parallel parable"—one which tells the same story using different or more modern objects, language, locations, and people, as well as contemporary jobs and points of

Explanation and Adaptation	Program
sents symbolically a reality in another sphere." As the participants write, instruct them to concentrate on bringing out the main point of the parable and not on the allegorical details that they might see in Jesus' parable. For examples of "parallel parables," look at *The Cotton Patch Gospel*, by Clarence Jordan, available from Judson Book Store or from Koinonia Partners, Route 2, Americus, GA 31709. A shorter alternative to writing and reading the parables is to do impromptu narrated skits. Have some people (without preparation) act out the parable as it is read by the narrator. These skits move quickly and are often quite humorous when performed in this manner. You might want to explore with the participants their ideas as to how these requirements for the kingdom relate to God's grace.	view. Share these parables by reading them or acting them out and discussing their major points. The Sower—Matthew 13:3-9; Mark 4:2-9; Luke 8:4-8 The Tares Among Wheat—Matthew 13:24-30 The Unmerciful Servant—Matthew 18:21-35 The Laborers in the Vineyard—Matthew 20:1-16 The Marriage Feast—Matthew 22:1-14 The Ten Virgins—Matthew 25:1-13 The Talents—Matthew 25:14-30 The Good Samaritan—Luke 10:30-37 The Rich Fool—Luke 12:16-21 The Lost Sheep—Luke 15:3-7 The Prodigal Son—Luke 15:11-32 The Pharisee and the Publican—Luke 18:9-14
	D. *Citizens of the Kingdom* Spend a few minutes as a group listing on newsprint the requirements for citizenship in this country. (Examples might be obeying the laws, being born here, taking an oath of allegiance, etc.) Then imagine that your group is the governing body of the kingdom of heaven. Referring to the Scriptures below and any others that might be helpful, write out on newsprint an official list of requirements for citizens of God's kingdom. Matthew 5:2-12; 6:1; 7:21; 18:1-4 Mark 1:15; 9:34 Luke 6:20-38; 18:15-17 John 15:12 Have the group reflect on both lists. How are they similar? How are they different?
Other options: 1. Have the participants write down the ways in which they meet or don't meet the requirements for citizenship in the kingdom. 2. List other persons who they feel	

Explanation and Adaptation	**Program**
meet the requirements for citizenship in the kingdom.	
You might want to facilitate this process by looking up examples of people yourself and bringing in articles, biographical sketches, or other sources that briefly tell their stories.	E. *The Value of the Kingdom* As a group, think of examples of historical as well as contemporary persons who have given their lives for the good of their country. This could be either through a life of service or death. Discuss what they gave up or sacrificed in their lives in order to do this (i.e., wealth, comfort, family, a future).
At this point, you may want to divide the group into pairs or small groups so that everyone will have a chance to share how these parables relate to his or her own life.	Now read Jesus' parables of the hidden treasure (Matthew 13:44) and the costly pearl (Matthew 13:45-46). Ask participants to compare and contrast the parables with the stories of the people they just mentioned. Next, have them share how they feel these parables speak to them. What is God asking them to do? Are they willing to give those things up for the kingdom? Is it a sacrifice or an opportunity?
This is an important and encouraging promise—don't let them miss it!	Have someone read Luke 18:18-30. Reflect together on the Good News that is contained in Jesus' promises (verses 27 and 29-30) for those who are willing to make sacrifices for God's kingdom.
Use a roll of paper or sheets of newsprint taped together to make the mural. If you are short on time, have each person create his or her own individual piece of the mural. If you have enough time, however, you may design a mural together and then join together in its creation.	F. *Kingdom Mural* As a group, design and make a mural that contains symbols of the kingdom of God, depicts scenes from Jesus' parables, lists kingdom words, or highlights individual citizens of the kingdom.
Flags and banners can be made out of paper as well as out of cloth.	Alternatives to making a mural would include making a "national" flag for the kingdom or putting together a banner that has significance for your group.
You might want to begin the mural or banner in this session and continue working on it over a period of time as a special project.	G. *Closing* Sit in a circle. Have everyone focus attention on the newsprint that lists the requirements for citizens of the kingdom of heaven (which should be placed in the cen-
This is the piece of newsprint that you worked on in section D of this session.	
If your group usually sings together,	

Explanation and Adaptation	Program
this would be an appropriate time for a few songs. If participants are keeping a journal, have them write down in it both the qualities that they have and the qualities that they want to develop as citizens of God's kingdom.	ter of the circle). Then, going around the circle, have each person say to the person sitting on the left something like, "A quality of kingdom citizenship that I see in you is _____." Now ask the group to spend a few minutes thinking about the qualities of citizens of the kingdom. Is there a quality that they want to develop more fully in their lives? After a few minutes of reflection invite the group to join with you in a time of prayer. You may choose to begin this time of prayer with an invitation to others to give their own prayers. After allowing time for those who wish to share, close with a few words.

God's Kingdom: One of Justice and Righteousness

J. W. Flair

Explanation and Adaptation	Program
	Objective:
	• To enable the participants to deepen their understanding of the concepts of justice and righteousness as they relate to New Testament teachings about the kingdom of God.
	Overview of the Session:
	A. Getting Started
	B. Rosalyn Righteous's Resumé
	C. People of the Kingdom
	D. Everyday Justice
	E. Skits About Kingdom Justice
	F. A Simulation—Judges of the Kingdom
	G. Closing
Some of the newsprint can be prepared ahead of time. Use an overhead projector or chalkboard if more convenient.	**Resources and Materials Needed:**
	Bibles, materials to make symbols of righteousness (cardboard, clay, papier-maché, Styrofoam), newsprint, markers.
	The Session in Detail:
Use your imagination and the resources available to you in creating the symbols. Some possibilities might be to make the symbols out of cardboard, clay, papier-maché, or Styrofoam.	A. *Getting Started*
	As participants enter the room, have them work in groups creating one of the three symbols of righteousness listed below. Have them spend a few minutes reading the Scripture given as an aid in determining why that object is symbolic of righteousness. When all have finished, have them share their creations and findings with the larger group. Display the symbols in the room.
	Crown of righteousness—2 Timothy 4:5-8
	Breastplate of righteousness—Ephesians 6:10-15

Explanation and Adaptation	Program

Fruit of righteousness—Hebrews 12:9-11

B. *Rosalyn Righteous's Resumé*
Working individually or in pairs, read the following Scriptures:

Matthew 5:6, 10, 20
Matthew 6:1
Matthew 25:31-40
Luke 12:22-34
Romans 1:16-17; 8:10
Ephesians 4:24–5:1
Philippians 3:7-16
1 Peter 3:8-14
1 John 2:28-29

The object here is to use a biblical basis and the participant's own concepts of Christian righteousness to create what they believe to be a model Christian.

Then, as a group, use your imagination and the Scriptures that were just read as the basis for writing a resumé for Rosalyn Righteous, who is applying for the job of "The World's Most Perfect Person." Bring Rosalyn to life by setting up the resumé on newsprint as follows:

If yours is a large group, you might choose to divide into smaller groupings with each group developing a resumé for Rosalyn.

Name: Rosalyn Righteous
Age:
Hometown:
Education:
Life Goals and Objectives:

Personal Qualities:

An option: After filling out the resumé, choose someone to play the part of Rosalyn and have the rest of the group interview her (or him—Ronald) for the job.

Previous Employment:
Hobbies and Other Activities:

A Personal Experience from Life (that demonstrates the applicant's righteousness):

You might also give participants a few minutes to reflect silently or on paper about what they would or would not write on the resumé about themselves.

After the group has filled out the resumé, spend a few minutes looking it over and see if you can get the entire group to agree that the Rosalyn of the resumé is the world's most perfect person.

C. *People of the Kingdom*
In pairs, look at the following Scripture passages that tell of people who were treated unjustly. How did these people react to the unjust treatment? What emotions did they display? Were their reactions those of citizens of the kingdom? Why? Share the findings and viewpoints with the larger group.

Stephen   Acts 7:54-60
Paul in Prison   Ephesians 1; 6:19-20

Explanation and Adaptation	Program

	Philippians 1:12-14, 18-21
Jesus	John 19:28-40,
	Luke 23:33-34
Barnabas and Paul	Acts 14:1-7
Jesus' Follower	Mark 14:43-52

If participants are not comfortable sharing about their own mistakes, then have them share about situations in which other people did something wrong toward them or tell general stories about people who failed to act as they should have.

D. *Everyday Justice*
In groups of two or three, have participants share some personal experiences in which they did something that they and others considered to be wrong, and the reaction of the person in charge (i.e., parent, teacher, police). How did they feel about the way they were treated? How did they feel about the particular punishment (or lack of punishment) they received? Did they feel that justice was done? If Jesus were the one handling each case, what would he have done?

If you have puppets or would like to make them, you can use them as an option for presenting the parables and stories. Another option is to act out modern versions of the parables and stories.

E. *Skits About Kingdom Justice*
Choose some or all of the following Bible stories and parables to be presented as skits by small groups. Allow each of the groups some time to read the story and create a short skit. Have each small group present its skit to the rest of the participants. After all the skits have been presented, discuss the kind of justice that was displayed in that account.

See if the participants can label the kind of justice described, for example: an eye for an eye, mercy, revenge, correction, and so on.

The Two Debtors—Luke 7:40-50
The Rich Man and Lazarus—Luke 16:19-31
The Prodigal Son—Luke 15:11-32
The Unmerciful Servant—Matthew 18:21-35
The Laborers in the Vineyard—Matthew 20:1-16
The Adulterous Woman—John 8:1-11

After each group has shared its skit, ask participants to share new learnings or understandings about justice.

To make these situations come alive, appoint a judge, lawyers for each side to argue the case, a jury, friends of the defendant, and so on. The lawyers should be given time to develop their cases. A second option would be to divide into

F. *A Simulation—Judges of the Kingdom*
Imagine that your group is the highest judicial body in the "Kingdom of God"—an all-Christian country that exists on the earth. Using the Bible as your "Constitution" and "Bill of Rights," you must decide what to do in the following situations.
1. A citizen named Joe has committed a murder. He has been found guilty and a lower court has sen-

Explanation and Adaptation	**Program**

Explanation and Adaptation

groups and have the group members work together to develop the case.

You might choose to do only one situation during the session and use the others at another time. An additional option would be to take one situation and have persons gather additional information and spend an entire session on that issue.

For more information on the death penalty write: The National Coalition Against the Death Penalty, 1501 Cherry Street, Philadelphia, PA 19102.

For more information on peace concerns write: Baptist Peace Fellowship of North America, 222 East Lake Drive, Decatur, GA 30030.

Program

tenced him to death. As the highest court in the land, you are to decide: Is the decision of the lower court "constitutional"? Is that decision violating any of Joe's rights as a citizen of the kingdom?

2. Many people are pouring over the borders into the kingdom because it is such a great place to live. They are coming at such a fast rate that some experts are warning that in a few years the resources of the kingdom will be unable to support all the people that will be living there. The politicians have voted to stop all people from coming in over the borborders. You must decide: Is the new law "constitutional"?

3. A country that seems hostile to the kingdom has weapons that are capable of destroying it at any time. The kingdom politicians are afraid that the other country might decide to use the weapons to destroy or take over the kingdom. Therefore, they have passed a law which calls for building the same weapons that the other country possesses in the hope that it will scare off the other country or produce a stalemate. However, the money to build the weapons will have to come from the money normally used to provide housing, food, and education for the people in the kingdom. If this money is used for weapons, some people in the kingdom will not have enough food and/or adequate housing and education. You decide: Is it "constitutional" to build the weapons? Is it violating the rights of the citizens to take away some of the money that they need for food, shelter, and education?

G. *Closing*

Have participants sit in a circle. Ask them to reflect on today's session and share a new learning or affirmation they gained today about justice and righteousness.

Now ask persons to think about their community, their homes, and their friends and lift up places where justice and righteousness are needed. Lift these concerns in prayer, asking for God's help in bringing justice and righteousness to your community.

Covenant
Soozi Whitten Ford

Explanation and Adaptation	Program

Having a variety of Bible translations will add to learnings in this session.
 	
The library of your pastor or your church is a good source for these books. Also check your public library or, if available, a local seminary library.
	Objectives:
	• To become familiar with covenants and the idea that covenants are a foundation for relationships.
	• To study the covenant at Sinai and other selected Old Testament covenants.
	
	Overview of the Session:
	A. Leader's Preparation
	B. Getting Started
	C. Developing the Session
	   1. Searching the Scriptures
	   2. Looking at the covenant at Sinai
	   3. Interview with Moses
	D. Reflection and Closing
	E. Evaluation
	
	Materials and Resources Needed:
	Bibles, journals or paper, pens, markers, newsprint, Bible dictionaries and encyclopedias. The following are some suggested resources: *Interpreter's Dictionary of the Bible, Vol. I* (Nashville: Abingdon Press, 1962); *Zondervan Pictorial Encyclopedia of the Bible* (Grand Rapids: Zondervan Publishing House, 1974); *Unger's Bible Dictionary* (Chicago: Moody, 1961).
	
	The Session in Detail:
	
	A. *Leader's Preparation*
	   1. Before the session, ask someone to play the part of Moses. Ask the person to be familiar with Exodus 19–24. Ask him or her to think about how Moses would have responded as a leader and how he would have felt about being the recipient of this

An "authentic" costume and make-up would greatly enhance this activity. Moses might be someone who is not a member of your group but who	

Explanation and Adaptation	Program

would be willing to participate in the session.

Adapted from *The Interpreter's Dictionary of the Bible, Vol. I* (Nashville: Abingdon Press, 1962), p. 714.

covenant on behalf of the people. The person playing Moses might also look at the questions suggested in "Interview with Moses," in section C.

2. You may find some of the following information helpful in supplementing your knowledge of covenants: A covenant is a solemn promise bound by an oath. The oath may be formed by either a verbal ritual (spoken promise, for example) or symbolic action (sharing a meal together, for example). The ritual or action is recognized by the parties involved as the act that obligates them to fulfill their agreement. A covenant establishes a *relationship* between two parties where one did not exist before.

An option would be to have persons work individually and report their learnings, or work together as one team.

B. *Getting Started*
1. Have Bible dictionaries and encyclopedias available on a table or shelf. Have persons work in teams of two or three persons. Encourage participants to do research on covenants using the resources you have made available. Some questions to guide their search might be:
   • What is a covenant?
   • How are covenants made?
   • Who makes covenants?

If your meeting space allows, post newsprint for future reference.

2. Have each team make notes on newsprint to share with the rest of the group. Allow time for each team to share its learnings.

C. *Developing the Session*
Provide a transition to the Bible study by summarizing some of the discoveries made above. Be affirming of the various contributions that were made. If you feel it is appropriate, include information from "Leader's Preparation" to supplement the learnings from the group work.
1. Searching the Scriptures
Working in pairs, learners examine several Scripture references. Ask each pair to share with the total group their responses to these questions:

If participants are keeping journals, suggest that they make charts to record information for future reference. Or, using newsprint, make one large chart for group reporting.

   • Who is involved in this covenant?
   • What relationship is established?
   • What are the conditions (requirements) of this covenant?
   • What is promised if the conditions are met?

Bible
Ref.   Who Conditions Promise

   Genesis 21:22-24—Abraham and Abimelech
   Genesis 31:43-55—Laban and Jacob

Explanation and Adaptation	Program
	Joshua 24:14-28—Joshua and the people 1 Samuel 18:1-4; 20:1-23—David and Jonathan Genesis 9:1-17—God and Noah Genesis 15:18; 17:1-11, 15-22—God with Abraham and Sarah Numbers 25:10-13—God and Phineas Isaiah 59:21—God and Israel 2 Chronicles 23:16-21—Jehoiada and the people
This is not intended to be an exhaustive list of covenants found in the Old Testament. Rather, these are examples of the many covenants found there. As you are preparing this session, you may prefer to substitute other passages for those suggested here. If time is short, these reflections may be omitted.	Allow participants to reflect on these passages privately. Which situation would they like to have been involved in? Which covenant would be the easiest for them to participate in? Which would be the most difficult? Why?
	2. Looking at the covenant at Sinai In Exodus 19–24, we find the record of Moses receiving the Ten Commandments from God on Mt. Sinai. You may know this passage by a number of different names, such as the Law, the Ten Commandments, the Old Covenant, the covenant at Sinai, the Mosaic covenant, and so on. Perhaps the variety of names indicates the importance of this covenant in our spiritual history. The following outline is a suggested way of looking at this passage.
Although it is best to study a passage in its context, time may not allow for a group reading of the entire Exodus 19–24 section. The outline is offered as a way to summarize the passage. As groups are preparing for their interview with Moses, you might suggest that they skim through the additional laws in Exodus 21–23 to get an idea of what is contained there.	Exodus 19:14-15—The people prepare themselves (preparation). Exodus 19:4-6—Moses recounts God's deliverance (remembering). Exodus 20:2-17—God's will is proclaimed (guidelines for life). Exodus 19:8; 24:3—The people pledge obedience to God (response). Exodus 24:1-11—Sacrifice is offered (celebration of the covenant relationship).
The outline has been adapted from *The Covenants in Faith and History*, by Stephen Szikszai (Philadelphia: Geneva Press, 1968), pp. 42–43.	3. Interview with Moses Allow participants, in groups of three or four, to design two or three questions that they would like to ask Moses about this covenant. Some of the following questions could be offered if a group needs guidance:
If you have access to video equipment, try taping Moses as he talks about the covenant and its importance. If this is done before your session, then the video could be played and questions could come from the presentation and be done as a group discussion instead of an interview.	• Why do you (Moses) think this covenant is so special?

Explanation and Adaptation	Program
	• Why did God choose a covenant to form a relationship between God and the people? • What is your favorite part of these laws? • Which ones will be the most difficult for you to follow?
Some other questions might be generated as a result of this process. If so, allow time for these as well.	When groups have designed their questions, return to the larger group. The person who is portraying Moses should join your session at this time. Allow individuals to interview Moses informally. Summarize by asking the group for observations and learnings.
This is private work and does not have to be shared with another unless the individual chooses to do so.	D. *Reflection and Closing* In journals or on paper, learners are encouraged to make a covenant with God for one week in which each individual decides on the conditions of the covenant. Some suggestions might be: cut TV viewing time in half for one week, make an honest attempt to be kind to mother/father/sister/brother/teacher, spend time each day in prayer and meditation, agree to volunteer time in service to the church, neighborhood, or community organization, and so forth.
Alternative closing: Allow participants to design a group covenant symbolized by verbal (chant) and symbolic (hugs or special handshake) ritual.	In a circle have the group repeat the following phrases after a leader enthusiastically: We are God's people . . . called together . . . to grow . . . to share . . . and to covenant . . . We are God's people! Amen and amen!
	E. *Evaluation* What parts of the session seemed to go well? What parts needed more work? Make notes in the margin of these things and other suggestions you may have to improve the session the next time you use this material.

New Covenant
Soozi Whitten Ford

Explanation and Adaptation	Program
	Objectives: • To be exposed to the idea that the New Covenant in Jeremiah 31:31-34 calls for a relationship to be established between God (through Jesus Christ) and people of faith (Christians). • To celebrate our covenant relationship with God through Jesus Christ.

	Overview of the Session:
	A. Leader's Preparation
	B. Getting Started
	C. Developing the Session
	   1. Seeing the message within
	   2. Searching the Scripture
	D. Closing Worship
	E. Evaluation

If you have not used the word "covenant" with your group, you might wish to use it in your preparation for this session.	Materials and Resources Needed: Bibles, journals or paper, pens, markers, newsprint, Communion elements.
An alternative would be to begin by sharing briefly about covenants in the Old Testament.	The Session in Detail: A. *Leader's Preparation* Read through the session plan and become familiar with the Scripture passages. Gather the necessary resources. If you intend to share in the Lord's Supper at the end of the session, you might want to invite your pastor or other staff person to join the group at that time. B. *Getting Started* Review the major learnings and activities from the previous session, especially for those who were unable to

Explanation and Adaptation	Program
	attend. If the newsprint work is still available, this would be an excellent way to review. What new insights were gained about covenants since the last session? In what way did the study allow participants' relationships with others to be viewed in a different light? Allow time for these questions and for inviting those who wish to share about their "covenant experience" to do so.
	C. *Developing the Session*
	1. Seeing the message within Use some of the following thoughts to lead your group in the activity.
	"We all have 'messages' that are indelibly printed in our hearts and guide our lives. We might call these our life philosophies, guidelines, or codes for living. Somehow, they provide continuity for the way we approach living and choosing."
Some quiet and soothing music may facilitate concentration. You may also use this as a guided imagery exercise. The hope here is to encourage group members to think of the positive "messages" within themselves. Be sensitive to youth who are experiencing negative messages such as "I am unlovable," "I cannot achieve," "I am a failure" and so on. Try not to force anyone to express a feeling that is not true for him or her.	While they are sitting comfortably or perhaps lying on the floor, have participants envision their "messages" within. Their messages might be "I am lovable and capable," "God loves me," "I am responsible," "I can choose and decide," and so on. Allow several minutes for participants to get their messages in focus. Then have each person draw his or her message and design on a blank journal page or on newsprint. Share the creations with the larger group using this formula: "I am _____(name)_____ and my message is _____."
If your group is so large that this sharing activity would be cumbersome, suggest sharing in groups of four to six.	If newsprint is used, post these in your meeting place as a way of declaring identity.
Different translations of the Bible may be helpful here.	2. Searching the Scriptures Have participants, in small groups of three or four, read the "new covenant" passage found in Jeremiah 31:31–34. Encourage groups to discover the meanings of this passage by using some of the following questions: • Who is involved in this covenant? • Who are "the house of Israel"? • What are the conditions of this covenant? • What is promised? • What relationship is established?
The thought here is that God wants us to know we are God's people and have that message written on our hearts so that it continually influences and guides our lives.	

Explanation and Adaptation	Program

If you used the chart from "Searching the Scriptures" in the previous session, you may choose to add these learnings on that chart.

If your group is small, you may prefer to divide in half and have one group working on each covenant. The chart could then be used for reporting in the larger group.

If your group is using journals, they may wish to record this chart there.

Be sensitive to those persons in your group who have not made an initial commitment to Jesus Christ as Lord and Savior.

The hope is that this activity will help learners to see that through a relationship with Jesus Christ Christians can know God and have God's law "written upon their hearts."

Allow a few moments for groups to share their learnings with the larger group. Be encouraging and affirming of all contributions.

Have participants return to the small groups with a sheet of newsprint and a marker. Instruct the learners to discover the advantages and disadvantages of both the old and the new covenants. The following chart may be used by each group to record thoughts and discoveries. Some thoughts are suggested, but encourage the groups to work on their own first.

	Advantages	Disadvantages
Old Covenant (Exodus 19–24)	written for all to see	too many detailed laws to remember Cumbersome to carry around
New Covenant (Jeremiah 31: 31-34)	can be called to mind at will becomes part of one's lifestyle	A relationship with God must be established in order to receive the new covenant, and therefore some persons will not be included.

Ask for learnings to be shared in the larger group, perhaps posting each group's newsprint as part of the reporting process.

Continue this portion of the Bible study by sharing the following information in your own words: "Although the new covenant in Jeremiah is made between God and the 'house of Israel' (usually understood to be persons of the Jewish faith), we find in the New Testament that as believers in Christ (Christians) we are also 'heirs according to promise' (Galatians 3:29). In other words, the new covenant is also intended for us! As we establish ourselves in relationship with Jesus Christ and continue to grow in discipleship, we come to know God as was promised in Jeremiah 31:34.

Take a few moments and allow groups to discover how the new covenant was instituted by Jesus during the Last Supper. Divide into four groups (or more if necessary), assigning one passage to each group.

Matthew 26:26-29
Mark 14:22-26
Luke 22:14-20
1 Corinthians 11:23-26

Explanation and Adaptation	Program
	• What is the setting for this passage? • How is the "new covenant" concept used here? • What idea is Jesus trying to get across to the disciples? Suggest that the small groups share their learnings with the larger group. Ask for observations and summaries. D. *Closing Worship* Using the following outline, encourage your group to design a worship service to celebrate their covenant relationship with God. The outline may be used as the order of worship. Suggest that groups be responsible for one focus of the service. The activities listed should only serve to spark imagination. Encourage creativity! Preparation: Provide an atmosphere to enable participants to focus on the worship experience. Gather "objects of meaning" used in this study—journals, newsprint, and so on. Provide background music. Remembering: Lead the community through a "remembering journey," calling to mind the activities and learnings from the two sessions. Remember other moments of learning enjoyed by this group. Guidelines for life: Lead the group in a journal activity. "As a covenant person, I will _____." Encourage persons to paraphrase the Ten Commandments and the new covenant into a new guide for life. Response: Create a group responsive reading. Encourage others to covenant together in small groups of two or three or in the large group. Communion: Share together in the Lord's Supper with particular emphasis on being the recipients of the new covenant through a relationship with Jesus Christ. E. *Evaluation* What new learnings were evidenced in this session? What work needs to be done to provide further clarification?

Solving the Puzzle
Clara E. Wong

Explanation and Adaptation	Program
	Objective: • To help participants discover and appreciate the historical development of the concept of the Trinity. Overview of the Session: A. Beginning the Session B. "A Clear Story" game C. The New Testament Story: Looking at the Scriptures D. Life from Inside a Soda Can E. Development of Historical Models F. The Words That Seem to Work G. Is the Puzzle Solved for You? Resources and Materials Needed: Cardboard to make signs, a bell, markers, Bibles, an empty soda can, newsprint, red tape or red ribbon. The Session in Detail: A. *Beginning the Session* Tell the group that this session will call upon their creative imagination and thoughtful attention because today we will explore the development of the concept of the Trinity. In the process, we plan to have fun!
Make up other situation sentences if you wish. Try to construct a well-defined situation that is short but open-ended.	B. *"A Clear Story" game* Situation sentences: 1. One dreary morning Elizabeth decided to brave the weather and take a letter she had written to the mailbox at the end of the block. 2. Two minutes to get down the concourse! In a few moments Arthur would see his best friend, whom he hadn't seen since the accident in the spring. 3. If Sidney hurried quickly through the garden, Mrs.

Explanation and Adaptation	Program
	Michaels and the girls at the party would never know he'd been spying on them.
Two is the minimum number. Use four teams if the group is very large. Reminder: watch the overall time for this session.	Divide the group into two teams. Give each team three pieces of blank cardboard and markers. Ask them to write a person on one, a place on the second, and a thing on the third. Have each team appoint three persons to keep the cardboard signs face down until signaled to raise one high in the air. Ask them to designate an order for the three persons to stand during the game.
	Object of the game: to weave the most credible story that is in keeping with the plot of the situation sentence and to use the words on the pieces of cardboard at the juncture of the story when a word is raised high in the air.
If you don't have a bell, decide on another sound signal.	How the game is played: The two teams sit facing each other. One team is selected to be the "storyteller" team; the other, the "facts" team. One person from the "storyteller" team will begin weaving a story, beginning with one of the situation sentences, and will continue until you ring the bell. At this point he or she will tag another team member and then one of the "facts" team will hold up a card. The new storyteller must use the fact to continue the story. Repeat this process until all three "facts" have been used. Give the final storyteller thirty seconds to complete the story after the last cardboard sign has been raised in the air.
	At the end of a story, the facts team may challenge the use of their words in the story. The storyteller team should be encouraged to think of a better way of weaving that word into the story line.
	Switch teams and try another situation sentence.
	C. *The New Testament Story: Looking at the Scriptures* Have participants work in two groups. Assign the first set of biblical passages to the first small group and the second set of Scriptures to the second. • Set 1: Romans 8:11; 2 Corinthians 4:14; Galatians 1:1; Ephesians 1:20; 1 Timothy 1:2; 1 Peter 1:21; and 2 John 1:9. • Set 2: Matthew 28:19; 1 Corinthians 6:11 and 12:4-5; Galatians 3:11-14; Hebrews 10:29; and 1 Peter 1:2. Bring the groups back together and have them share which members of the Trinity (God; Jesus Christ, the

Explanation and Adaptation	Program
	Son of God; the Holy Spirit) are mentioned together.
	These passages indicate that there was no fixed wording. Although an understanding of a three-part Godhead was present even in this early period, no cohesive doctrine for the Trinity was presented.
	During the following centuries the church tried to work through the implications of the doctrine of the Trinity. The church had the strong proclamation of one true God in the Old Testament, and it had the joyous Good News of Jesus' life, death, and resurrection in the New Testament. It was trying to explain clearly how this one God, Jesus Christ, and the Holy Spirit fit together. The basic story was certain. Questions about the details were another matter, particularly in the face of questioning by pagans.
	In some sense it is like the story game we played. We know how the story begins, and we think we know where we are headed. Certain facts are part of the story, but it's not always clear how they "work" in the story.
You could make a large picture of an empty soda can to place in the center of the room.	D. *Life from Inside a Soda Can* With the whole group together, bring out an empty soda can and place it where it is visible. Draw on newsprint a large circle with a wedge (the hole on the top rim). Darken the circle except for the wedge. Explain that this is what you would see if you lived inside a soda can: one wedge of light to the outside world.
	Ask the participants to imagine being inside a soda can. How could they figure out what the world outside the soda can was like? Write their spontaneous responses on newsprint. Try to encourage an imaginative and playful spirit.
In the first few centuries important features of the Christian faith were set down. Options in belief and practice were either accepted or rejected. Believers developed a sense of worship, communal life, and relatedness to other communities of faith. During this time they evolved a vocabulary for their beliefs. This vocabulary tried to describe who God is.	After they have given some responses, ask them to consider how their attempts are similar to learning about God. God is more than our limited conclusions about our world and this universe, and yet somehow God is present to us in our "soda cans."
	Defining God from our limited experience is hard. People of the early church had their work cut out for them.

Explanation and Adaptation	Program
	E. *Development of Historical Models*

Draw this diagram on a piece of newsprint.

```
                    SUBORDINATIONISM
                         /\
                        /  \
                       /    \
                      /      \
                     /        \
                    /   GOD    \
                   /  (Three in  \
                  /     One)      \
     MODALISM    /_____\   TRITHEISM
```

From the second century through the fourth century, the church struggled to define how God, Jesus Christ, and the Holy Spirit make up the Godhead. How are they related to one another? How can they be the same and be different? Do they have different functions?

Here are some theories that have been rejected:

Print these definitions on newsprint and add beside the first diagram.

- *Subordinationism:* Jesus was a man who was adopted by God to be the Son of God. He became part of the Trinity after his resurrection.
- *Modalism* (also called Monarchianism or Sabellianism): God was first God the Creator, then became Jesus Christ, and is present as Spirit to us. God expresses a presence in one of the three options at any given time.
- *Tritheism:* God is actually three separate gods in one.

Without diminishing God as the one and only God, can we understand how Jesus Christ and the Holy Spirit fit in? How do we integrate the doctrine of the Trinity into a monotheistic faith?

What clues and traces do we see of God's presence with us? Is God different at different times in our lives? Is God changeable? Is God always the same? Ask them to share their feelings.

If you plan to use session 9, you might want to write their ideas on newsprint in order to compare their feelings later.

Draw this diagram on a piece of newsprint.

F. *The Words That Seem to Work*

```
                 Creator
          is not  |      is not
            \     is     /
             \    |     /
              \  God   /
          is\    /  \    /is
             \  /    \  /
     Jesus Christ __is not__ Holy Spirit
```

Explanation and Adaptation	Program
	This is how the Trinity has been understood since the fifth century. This is the classical trinitarian formula.
homoousios—"the same substance" *homoiousios*—"of like substance"	The Eastern bishops were unhappy about the concept of *homoousios* and preferred the concept of *homoiousios* to describe the Trinity. A group of Eastern bishops called the Cappadocians showed the entire Eastern church how to interpret *homoousios* in light of *homoiousios*.
	Agreements were reached through the work of these Cappadocians, and in A.D. 381 the Council of Constantinople united to affirm the doctrine of the Trinity:
Write these statements on newsprint.	• All three have one substance. • The Godhead exists simultaneously in three modes of being.
	G. *Is the Puzzle Solved for You?*
	Ask the group if the final form is clear for them. What do they like about the formula? What is unclear or puzzling for them?
Option: Print the Nicene Creed on newsprint.	Hand out a copy of the Nicene Creed, which affirms the doctrine of the Trinity as experienced by humankind. Ask participants to think about this declaration of faith for next time.

We believe in one God,
    the Father, the Almighty,
    maker of heaven and earth,
    of all that is, seen and unseen.
 We believe in one Lord, Jesus Christ,
 the only Son of God,
 eternally begotten of the Father,
 God of God, Light from Light,
 true God from true God,
 begotten not made,
 of one Being with the Father.
 Through him all things were made.
 For us and from our salvation
    he came down from heaven:
 by the power of the Holy Spirit
    he became incarnate from the Virgin Mary,
    and was made man.
 For our sake he was crucified under Pontius Pilate:
    he suffered death and was buried.
    On the third day he rose again in accordance with the Scriptures;
    he ascended into heaven
    and is seated at the right hand of the Father.	

Explanation and Adaptation	Program

He will come again in glory to judge
the living and the dead,
and his kingdom will have no end.
We believe in the Holy Spirit, the
Lord, the giver of life,
who proceeds from the Father
and the Son.
With the Father and the Son
he is worshiped and
glorified.
He has spoken through the
Prophets.
We believe in one holy catholic
and apostolic Church.
We acknowledge one baptism for
the forgiveness of sins.
We look for the resurrection
of the dead,
and the life of the world to
come. Amen.[1]

[1]*Book of Common Prayer*, 1977, Church Hymnal
Corporation, Seabury Press, N.Y., N.Y.

Session **9**

I See You
Clara E. Wong

Explanation and Adaptation	Program
	Objectives: • To help participants explore a fuller appreciation of the Trinity in their lives. • To expand an understanding of the Trinity as the presence of God among us. **Overview of the Session:** A. Skits B. Who's Who? C. Character Sketches D. Who Fits the Bill? E. Anybody You Know? F. Implications **Materials Needed:** Newsprint and markers.
Have a local acting group come in to perform each of the three parts of the Trinity. Ask session participants to name what they saw in the skits, who was being played, and what acts were performed.	**The Session in Detail:** A. *Skits* Divide participants into three working groups. Assign one group to be God the Father, another Jesus Christ, and the third the Holy Spirit. Ask each group to work independently and create a short pantomime to present to the whole group that tells who they are and what they do. Ask them to be as specific as they can be in their acting. Assemble the participants and watch the skits. After all the skits have been performed, ask for their reactions. B. *Who's Who?* Divide the participants again into small groups. Give

Explanation and Adaptation	**Program**
	them some newsprint and markers and ask them to brainstorm about the Trinity. Ask them to make two columns: one titled "Shared or common aspects" and the other, "Special or unique aspects." Bring the group back together to share their discoveries with one another.
	C. *Character Sketches* Divide a piece of newsprint into three columns or put up three pieces of newsprint side by side. Write "God," "Jesus Christ," and "Holy Spirit" over the columns.
These should be characteristics and not merely names we ascribe to God.	With the agreement of the group, begin to summarize a character sketch for each person of the Trinity. The responses might be:

God	**Jesus**	**Holy Spirit**
bring to life	Redeemer	comfort
creates	Savior	unites
eternal	one of us	restores
omnipresent	healer	leads
omnipotent	teacher	explain
love	confronts	God's mind
merciful		to us

	These words help us to understand the Trinity in our lives and throughout our history. For us, the Trinity is not so much a formula that protects the oneness of God as it is a way of defining God's presence among us.
	D. *Who Fits the Bill?* Ask the group members to think of and describe famous men and women who exemplify each member of the Godhead. If they have difficulty, suggest that they think about such figures as Martin Luther King, Jr., Nathan the prophet to David, Lincoln, Bishop Tutu, John the Baptist, Lionel Richie, Mother Teresa, Harriet Tubman, and so on.
Write these characteristics on newsprint and compare them with the list made in section C.	E. *Anybody You Know?* Ask for volunteers to tell about special people in their lives who have made God real to them. Ask them to name some of the characteristics they felt were present in that person which brought the presence of God close to them.
	The people who are mentioned may seem to share characteristics that we attribute to the Trinity. They may give some of us the feeling and recognition of God's presence among us, and yet each person has done something different.

Explanation and Adaptation	**Program**
	We see that the Trinity, which we learned about in the last session, is one God with simultaneous modes of being or expression who can be seen through special people. God is not far away but very close.
	F. *Implications* Can we say then that an artist who creates a breathtaking painting or a musician who touches our feelings through music or a writer who helps us think and see and feel more keenly brings God's presence close to us?
If we can better understand God's presence through creation and other living beings, what does this say about how we live together in God's world?	When someone shows us a new understanding of God or he or she says just the right thing to heal an old wound or help change you for the better, is not God in the midst of us?
	When someone comforts you when nothing seems to work or when a friend helps you heal a broken relationship, is not God as close as breath to us?
	The presence of God surrounds us, even when we do not comprehend it. The Trinity is not some abstract formula but, rather, a shorthand way of stating something we can feel in our lives.
	The fullness of God's presence among us is not any less than when Moses faced the burning bush or when the Hebrews walked on dry land in their exodus from Egypt or when Jesus himself was a human being on this earth or when the tongues of fire descended at Pentecost. We live in the midst of God's full presence, and God's presence lives within us, waiting for the flames of the Spirit to ignite our lives into new life for all to see.

Sin in the World

Jeff Jones

Explanation and Adaptation	Program
	Objectives: • To enable youth to develop an understanding of the reality of sin in the world. • To help youth develop an awareness of the biblical understanding of sin. **Overview of the Session:** A. Agree/Disagree Statements B. Types of Sins—Bible Study C. Sin as Part of the Human Condition—Bible Study D. Contemporary Skits E. Conclusion **Resources and Materials Needed:** Bibles, newsprint, markers, props for use in the skit. **The Session in Detail:** A. *Agree/Disagree Statements* Ask group members to respond to the following statements. If they believe the statement is true, they move to one side of the room; if they believe it is false, they move to the other side of the room. After they have responded to each statement, ask them to share with someone why they believe as they do. Some may want to share with persons who agree with them, and others may share with those who disagree.
Add to or change any of these statements to include issues that you believe are significant for group members. The purpose of this exercise is not to get right answers but to begin the process of thinking and	all evil and suffering is caused by sin. Satan causes us to sin. God uses our sin to teach us about God's love. Jesus died for our sins. People continue to sin after becoming Christians. Sin is part of being human; we cannot escape it.

Explanation and Adaptation	Program
talking about sin. It is important to be open to all responses that youth share.	The type of sin we commit is different after we become Christians. Sin is not just personal; groups of people, societies, and nations can also sin. Sin is disobedience to the will of God. B. *Types of Sins—Bible Study* Write "Sins" at the top of a sheet of newsprint. Ask group members to call out all the types of sins they can think of. These may be both "major" (murder) and "minor" (not eating everything on your plate) sins—anything they have been told is wrong or a sin.
The quickest way to do this is to give a different passage to each person and then assign another as each finishes with his or her initial passage.	When the group has listed all the sins it can think of, assign the following passages to group members. Ask them to read the passages and call out the sins named. Write these on the newsprint, adding to the list the group has already begun. Exodus 20:1-17 Amos 2:6-8 Amos 5:10-13 Matthew 15:19 Luke 18:11 2 Corinthians 12:20 2 Timothy 3:2-4 Ephesians 4:25-31 Hosea 4:1-3 Jeremiah 2:4-13 Romans 1:28-31 Romans 13:13 Galatians 5:19-21 The list should be quite extensive by now. Suggest to the group that there are at least two ways in which we might respond to this list. We might feel overwhelmed by all the things we do that are considered sins. Or we might look at the list and feel pretty good because we don't do many (or most) of the things that are included (at least not very often). Ask group members what their feelings are, and discuss which of the two options comes the closest to their responses. C. *Sin as Part of the Human Condition—Bible Study* Explain to the group that the question of *how* sinful we are (in the sense of how many sins we commit) is not a major concern of the Bible. This is true because the Bible understands sin not only as specific action but also as a condition that is a part of all human life. Jesus talked about both of these views of sin.

Explanation and Adaptation	Program
	Ask group members to turn to Matthew 5:17-28. Ask them to read these verses and consider what Jesus was getting at in these words. Did he mean that it was a sin to be angry with someone, just as murder is a sin? Was he saying that all anger should be done away with, just as murder should be? Or was he trying to make another point? After this discussion suggest to the group that Jesus was trying to make the point that sin involves something more than just wrong actions.
These groups can be as small as two persons. These questions can be written out on cards or small pieces of paper and given to each group.	In order to help youth get a clearer insight into what Jesus had in mind, divide the group into four smaller groups and assign each group one of the passages listed below. Ask each group to focus its discussion around the questions listed after each passage. 1. Luke 15:11-23 (the prodigal son)—What was the sin of the older brother? He had stayed home and done all that his father asked. Was he as sinful as the younger brother? 2. Romans 7:14-20—Is the sin Paul talks about just the evil that he does or something else? How do you understand the phrase "So I am not really the one who does this thing; rather it is the sin that lives in me"? 3. Genesis 3:1-13 (the fall)—What does this story tell us about sin? What is the point that is made through the story? What do you understand the sin of Adam and Eve to have been? Was it the act of eating the fruit, or was there something more to their sin? What meaning do you get from the story? from the actions of the snake? from the actions of Adam and Eve? 4. Matthew 19:16-21 (the rich young ruler)—The young man had followed all of the commandments; his deeds were all good ones. In what way would he be considered a sinner? What was his sin? Allow about five minutes for the small groups to do their work. Then bring everyone back together and ask the groups to give brief reports of their answers to the questions. Have the following statement on newsprint so that all can see it. Read it and ask if this understanding of sin fits with what they read in the passage they studied. "Sin is a part of who we are as human beings. It is that part of us which keeps us separated from God and others, which keeps us from being the persons God intends for us to be."

Explanation and Adaptation	Program
These groups need only have four or five persons in them. If the group is too small to divide, have everyone work on one skit. This will mean that there will be no one to whom to present the skit, but they will still have the fun and learning of developing it. Other options for expressions besides skits include written stories, poems, pictures, or murals. These can be worked on individually, in small groups, or as an entire group together.	D. *Contemporary Skits* Divide the group into two groups. Explain that the task for each group will be to develop a skit based on one of the four passages that have just been studied. Indicate that the skit should be a contemporary version of one of the passages and that it should illustrate the concept of sin as part of who we are as persons rather than just as bad deeds that we do. Allow 15–20 minutes for preparation of the skits. Then have the groups share their creations. Encourage those watching to respond with enthusiastic affirmation of the presentation. The skits may speak for themselves so that no discussion following them may be necessary. If appropriate, however, take a few minutes to discuss the issues the skits raise after each of them is presented.
	E. *Conclusion* Take several minutes to review the major learnings that can come from this session: 1. The Bible sees sin both as acts (deeds) and as a condition of human life. 2. While there is a difference in the number of sinful deeds persons commit, all persons share in the sin that comes as part of being human. 3. Sin is as much a reality for contemporary life as it was in biblical times. Ask group members if they have any reactions to the work that they would like to share with others. Any questions?
Depending upon your group, this could be a shared prayer of confession.	Close the session with prayer, acknowledging the sin which is a part of all of our lives and for which the Bible's teachings offer us understanding and the hope of overcoming.

Sin in My Life
Jeff Jones

Explanation and Adaptation	Program
	Objectives: • To help youth consider the reality of sin in their own lives. • To consider biblical insights related to sin in our lives. Overview of the Session: A. Introduction B. Sin in the Christian Life C. Bible Studies on Sin D. Our Involvement in Sin E. Our Own Sin F. Closing Resources Needed: Bibles, newsprint, markers, paper, pencils. The Session in Detail: A. *Introduction* If you have done the "Sin in the World" session before this one, remind the group that its focus was on the reality of sin in the world and what the Bible has to say about it. Indicate that in this session the focus will be more personal; we will be considering the reality of sin in our own lives, our personal involvement in sin. Acknowledge that this may be difficult to do. Explain that although you hope there will be an openness in sharing with one another, no one will be pressured to share anything he or she does not wish to share. B. *Sin in the Christian Life* Have the following list written on newsprint. Explain that it offers several possible responses to the role of sin in the life of a Christian. As you read through the

Explanation and Adaptation	**Program**
	list, ask group members to vote on each. They are to raise their hands if they believe it is true, put thumbs down if they believe it is false, or just sit quietly if they do not have an opinion. After you have completed the list, ask group members to suggest additional options that may also be voted on. After we become Christians:
These statements are to stimulate thinking and discussion. Be careful to avoid judging opinions which group members have at this point.	• we try harder not to sin. • our sins are not as bad. • we know we are forgiven. • we no longer commit major sins. • our sin is about the same as before. • we have a greater sense of sin. • we can live a life that is almost free of sin. • we continue to share in the sin that society commits. • we need to do something about our sin. • we can sin more because we know Jesus Christ died for us already.

This discussion can also be with the entire group, especially if there are eight or fewer in the group.	When all the options have been voted on, ask group members to select the one (or two) that best describes their belief. Ask them to get together in groups of three persons to discuss why they chose the options(s) they did.
	
	C. *Bible Studies on Sin*
	Divide the group into three sections. Give each section one of the following passages. Each group is to read the passage and consider what insight it gives about sin in the lives of those who have encountered Christ and committed themselves to Christ:
	
	  1. Luke 22:54-62—Peter's denial
	  2. John 20:24-49—Thomas' doubt
	  3. 1 Corinthians 1:10-17; 5:1-9; 6:7-11—Paul's correspondence
	
	After the three reports have been shared, note that all of them serve as illustrations of the reality that we do not stop sinning after we become Christians. Now ask group members to consider: If this is true, what is the difference between the Christian sinner and the non-Christian sinner?

Explanation and Adaptation	Program
Note that the statements used in the previous step are possible ways in which the questions can be answered and that in this session you will be looking at insights the Bible brings to the question.	D. *Our Involvement in Sin* Suggest to the group that there are two significant reasons why a Christian continues to sin after she or he accepts Christ: 1. The process of working out our salvation—living as saved persons—is a long one that involves consistent work to change our life practices as we grow in relationship with God. Refer to Paul's statement in Philippians 2:12-13 in which he talks about working out our salvation "in fear and trembling."
These explanations might be easier to understand if you have the following written on newsprint: 1. It takes time and effort to change life practices as we grow in our relationship to God. 2. Sin is corporate as well as personal.	2. Since sin is corporate (that is, related to what groups or societies or nations do) as well as personal, we cannot escape our involvement in sin no matter how good our personal lives may be. If, for example, we are part of a society that practices racism, we in some sense participate in that sin, even though we may not think we are racists. Refer to Amos 2:6-8, explaining that in the passage Amos indicated that God held the entire nation responsible for sins even though not every individual had committed them. Indicate that this passage is just one of many in the Bible in which this sense of corporate sin is made clear.

Have the following list of sins on newsprint. Explain that the list contains both personal and corporate sins. Ask group members to write "Sins in My Life" at the top of a piece of paper and then list on the paper those sins in which they have participated. Note that the way we are involved in corporate sin may be different from the way we are involved in personal sin. What is important here, however, is our own sense of a sin being one in which we are involved either personally or through our participation in a group, society, or nation. Let the group members know that this work is personal and they will not be asked to share it with anyone.

selfishness	lying
pride	cheating
war	racism
oppressing others	sexism
robbery	slander
murder	greed
dishonesty	jealousy
vice	malice
deceit	envy
disobeying parents	gossip
drunkenness	insulting others

Explanation and Adaptation	Program

bitterness   boastfulness
conceit   violence
unkindness   idolatry (giving
honor to some-
thing other than God)

As they complete their lists, ask group members to spend some time in silent reflection about the sins that they have included.

E. *Our Own Sin*
Point out to the group that for Jesus the concern was always for the person to come to an awareness of his or her own sin. It did not matter how the person compared to others or what the list of sins included. What mattered was that the person recognize and do something about the sins that were his or hers.

Explain to the group that you will be reading the story of Jesus and the woman at the well. Ask them to listen as you read and try to put themselves in the place of the woman. Jesus said to her, "You have been married to five men and the man you live with now is not really your husband." Ask group members to consider what Jesus would say to them about their lives and how they live.

Read John 4:7-18 in a modern English translation such as the *Good News Bible*. When you finish, ask group members to take a few minutes to reflect upon what Jesus' words to them might be. Suggest that they might want to write some of their thoughts on the paper that they used earlier.

F. *Closing*
Ask the group to join with you in prayer. In the prayer acknowledge the difficulty we have in facing our sins even though we recognize that Jesus calls us to do so. If the level of sharing in the group is a significant one, you may want to allow time for sentence prayers from group members.

In closing, share with the group that the same Jesus who asked us to confront our sins also promised us forgiveness for those sins. This is one of the major differences for Christians as they deal with the reality of sin. Christians do so in the belief that in confronting and confessing their sins they will receive forgiveness and the opportunity to begin again.

Grace: Receiving God's Favor
Don Harrington

Explanation and Adaptation	Program
	Objectives: • To help participants discover that grace is God's loving-kindness and undeserved favor. • To help participants identify moments in their lives when they have received grace. • To enable participants to recognize ways in which God's loving grace may extend to others through them.
	Overview of the Session: A. Getting Started B. Comparing a Hymn and Scripture C. Case Studies D. A Biblical Study of Grace E. Celebration F. Closing
The gifts, newsprint, tape recording, and balloons will need to be prepared ahead of time.	Resources and Materials Needed: Bibles, inexpensive gifts (purchased or made), markers, newsprint, paper/pens, balloons, tape recorder.
	The Session in Detail:
An undeserved favor is something done for another with no strings attached.	A. *Getting Started* When the group has gathered, ask the members to pair up with another person. Have them spend a couple of minutes sharing the best "undeserved favor" someone has ever done for them. Then ask each pair to form a group with another pair and share with one another what their partners said. Have them discuss how it feels to receive an undeserved favor.
The leader may have to encourage conversation. Discuss, but be care-	Indicate to the group that the biblical name for an undeserved favor is grace. As a way of beginning to

Explanation and Adaptation	Program
ful not to give the impression that one answer is "the correct" one. This exercise is to encourage discussion and to show different beliefs that are held about grace.	think and share about grace, ask group members to respond to the following statements. If they feel the statement is false, they should move to one side of the room; if they feel the statement is true, they should move to the other side of the room. After they arrive on their side of the room, ask them to share with someone why they believe as they do. Have one or two persons from each side share some of these feelings with the whole group.
	• Grace means that God loves us with no strings attached.
	• The proper way to receive God's grace is to earn it by regularly attending worship and following God's rules.
	• God loves us only when we do good things.
	• God won't accept people who drink or abuse drugs.
	• God gives grace to all persons who accept it.
You may want to use another hymn that is more familiar to the persons in your group. Have the words already written on newsprint or have hymnals available. To help in formulating the group definition you might summarize the key concept of each pair (or triad) on another sheet of newsprint.	B. *Comparing a Hymn and Scripture* Ask the group members to work in pairs or triads. Have them compare the words to the hymn "Amazing Grace" with Ephesians 1:3-10 and formulate a definition of the term "grace." Print the words to "Amazing Grace" on newsprint and post them where all can see. Once they have a definition, have them share their definition with the group. Help the group decide upon a definition that includes everyone's ideas. Print that definition on newsprint and put it in a prominent place in the room.
You may want to substitute "grace" stories of which you may be aware.	C. *Case Studies* Pose the following question to the group: Should we give loving-kindness or undeserved favor to all people regardless of what they have done? Tell the group that you are now going to examine some case studies to explore this question further. Divide into three small groups. Assign each group a different case study:
Have each case study on a separate card so the group can refer to it during their discussion.	1. Jerry liked to party and used to try to go as far as he could with every girl he dated in college. After college he quickly married one girl with whom he got along well. After a few years of marriage, she had a nervous breakdown and they were divorced. In reaction to this experience, Jerry began to drink heavily and smoke marijuana. He would find a woman he liked and live with her for

Explanation and Adaptation	Program
	awhile, and then go on to another. Finally, he joined a church and was befriended by the pastor. Jerry quit drinking and drugs and has now decided to go into the pastoral ministry.
	2. Johnny was involved in a youth gang. Caught in the act of mugging a woman, he ran from the scene and was cornered by a police officer. He shot the officer but was caught by another police officer and sent to prison. Johnny's bullet had lodged in the first officer's spine and was not able to be removed. Because of the injury the officer could no longer work. While Johnny was in prison, he confessed his faith in Christ. After being paroled he returned to his old neighborhood and wanted to join a church. The injured police officer's parents and brothers are members of this church.
The case studies may help the group see how hard it is for us to understand that grace is undeserved and available for all.	3. Vicky was a heavy drug user in high school. Her drug habit led her to become a dealer. She sold drugs to many junior high and high school students. One night she had a bad experience with a hallucinogenic drug and was taken to her pastor's house. The pastor and Vicky struggled the whole night to help her overcome this experience. That night Vicky decided to give up drugs, both using and dealing. The next day she came forward in church to give her life to Christ. In church that day were the parents of a young man to whom she had sold drugs. He had had an accident in a car while under the influence of drugs and was disabled for life.
	Ask the group members to identify with each person in the study. How do they feel? How would they react? Should these persons receive grace? How would Christ have reacted in these situations?
	After each group has had enough time to read and discuss the studies, have them join together in a large group. Have each group share their situation and their reaction with the whole group. Allow time for others in the group to respond to each situation.
	D. *A Biblical Study of Grace* Tell the group you are going to investigate a biblical story about grace. The scene is Calvary, outside of Jerusalem. Jesus is on the cross with two thieves on crosses beside him. The crowd is gathered—

Explanation and Adaptation	Program
	bystanders, Pharisees, and families of those dying on the crosses.
Another option would be to stay together as a total group, asking each person to choose one of the perspectives from which to listen.	Have the group divide into four groups. Each group is to listen to the story from the perspective of one of the following: 1. a Pharisee—one who engineered the death of Christ 2. the mother of the professing thief 3. the mother of Jesus 4. the crowd
Ask five persons ahead of time to record the Scripture passage as a dramatic reading. The characters are the narrator, Jesus, a government official, a soldier, and the two thieves.	Play the tape of Luke 23:32-43 and allow time for brief reflection. Remind them that they are putting themselves in the shoes of another person. Ask the group members to share their feelings with others listening from the same perspective. Then allow time for the total group to share the different perspectives.
Personal grace stories should be shared only if individuals wish. These might be too personal to share with the total group.	Now ask the group to reflect on their own lives. Have there been times when they received grace? What were the circumstances? How did they feel? Did anyone feel they should not receive grace? After a time of silent reflection, ask if anyone would like to share his or her "grace" story with the group.
The balloons should be blown up ahead of time and, if possible, hidden until this part of the session. An option would be to have brief notes written and give a note to each person.	E. *Celebration* Write short messages on small pieces of paper and place them in balloons. Give each person in the room a balloon and have everyone stand in a circle and volley the balloons. After a few minutes, ask everyone to hold a balloon. This will not be the balloon that they started with. At the count of three have everyone sit on his or her balloon to find the "grace" message inside. Have group members read their messages.
	Share with the group that this was a fun way to get an unexpected gift. While we often think of gifts as something we buy, we can also give gifts to one another. One gift we can give is to share how we see one another extend grace to others. A second gift is to encourage one another to grow in gracefulness. Ask the group to mill around the room giving gifts of grace to each other.
As leader, try to speak to each person during the milling time. Be on the lookout for any person who seems to not be included.	F. *Closing* After the time of sharing come together as a total group. Reflect on the learnings from this session and restate that God's grace is a gift that is freely given to

Explanation and Adaptation	Program
This could be a time for first-time commitments or for commitments to be more forgiving, accepting, and so on. It would be helpful if the chairs for the first part of the closing activity were in a circle so that the group would just need to stand at this point.	all. Each of us chooses how to respond to this gift. Allow a few minutes for silent reflection. After the reflection time say that this may be a time when they want to respond in new ways to the gift of God's grace. After any commitment have the group respond, "We will be praying for you." Following the opportunity for commitment, have the group stand in a circle. Ask those who would like to, to share a sentence prayer thanking God for their learnings today. After all who wish to do so have shared, the leader, or designated persons, should close the prayer by saying: "And all the people said, 'Amen.'"

The Cross: Motivation for Discipleship

Don Harrington

Explanation and Adaptation	Program
This session could also be helpful in a group with persons who have not made an initial faith commitment.	Objectives: • To help participants understand that Christ's death on the cross was an expression of love for us. • To enable participants to examine ways that others have expressed their love for God. • To assist participants in discovering that they too are disciples and their discipleship should grow out of their acceptance of Christ's love for them. Overview of the Session: A Getting Started—The Hero/Heroine Game B. Pass the Potato C. Bible Discovery D. Sources of Motivation E. Historical Lovers of Christ F. In-Depth Bible Encounter G. Cross Bearing for One Another H. Closing—Prayer of Commission Resources and Materials Needed: Bibles (at least three different translations, such as RSV, TEV, NIV), paper, pencils or pens, bag of potatoes (enough for each person to have one), pieces of wood lath (i.e., 1 inch by 1/2 inch by 3 inches—enough for one for each person, including leader), newsprint, markers.
Begin the session with enthusiasm. These might include sports figures, rock singers, TV stars, government or church leaders, family members, and so forth.	The Session in Detail: A. *Getting Started—The Hero/Heroine Game* Ask the participants to divide into three small groups to hold a contest to see how many modern heroes and heroines they can name in three minutes. These persons must be ones with whom the youth of today identify.

Explanation and Adaptation	Program
	At the end of three minutes have each group post its list. Give time for others to see each list. Are there duplications on each list? Some persons who show on only one list? Allow a little time for others to ask why the group included a certain person or did not include a person.
If there are more than eight or ten persons in your group, you might want them to share with one other person. Another option would be to have persons who selected the same person to share with each other.	After the game is over, urge each person to select from any list a person with whom they can identify. Encourage them to explain why they chose that person.
Have fun with this exercise. Ham it up as you introduce it.	B. *Pass the Potato*
Try to select a bag of potatoes that has potatoes that have similar shapes and sizes.	Pass a bag of potatoes around and have each person select a potato. Say to the group, "All these potatoes are similar to one another. Take two minutes to get to know your potato. Look at its shape, its texture, its bumps, and any other special marks. Become well enough acquainted with your potato so you will be able to find it again.
Tell the persons to take their potato home and place it in a glass of water. As it grows during the next few weeks, it will be a reminder to them that disciples are called to grow.	After each person has examined a potato for two minutes, collect the potatoes again, mix them up (carefully, please), and place them on the table. Each person is to find his or her own personal spud. Discuss what helped each person pick out her or his own potato. What did they discover during the exercise and how can this learning relate to being a disciple? Summarize by saying that in order truly to know Jesus we must *identify* with Jesus, especially his experience on the cross.
Use any three translations that are available to you.	C. *Bible Discovery*
	Select persons to read the assigned Scripture passages from at least three different translations (i.e., RSV, TEV, NIV). The passages are: 2 Corinthians 5:14-20; 1 John 4:10-11; John 3:16; and John 10:17-18.
Try to set a dramatic scene so that the participants can step right into it.	Instruct the participants to imagine that they are the apostle Peter. It is a couple of days after Jesus of Nazareth has ascended to heaven. Peter is waiting for the coming of the Holy Spirit (Pentecost). After thinking for a while about the crucifixion, he sits down to write a letter to his father. In the letter Peter tries to explain why Jesus died on the cross and why he (Peter) is going to continue to spread the gospel.

Explanation and Adaptation	Program
You might want to divide the group in pairs or triads for writing the letters. Ask participants to listen carefully to the letters of others so that they can react to them.	Now ask the group members to write the letter, using the Scripture passages as background. After the writing is completed, request that each person (or small group) read the letter. Ask the other group members to react to the ideas presented in each letter. Once all have shared, summarize the ideas that have been expressed.

If the following ideas do not come out in the sharing, include them in your summary:
• The cross is God's love in concrete action.
• Our response to God's love is to love others.
• God initiated this process by loving us first, through Christ's death on the cross.
• Therefore, we now can respond in gratitude to God by loving others.

D. *Sources of Motivation*
What motivates us to action? Have the participants brainstorm all of the things that could motivate a person to action.

Present the following rules for the brainstorming:

1. Give suggestions as quickly as possible.
2. Give any ideas that come to mind.
3. Don't evaluate individual responses. |
| Print the list on newsprint as they are shared. Two writers will help in capturing the group's quick responses. | Prime the pump if necessary. Make sure these factors are included in the list:

1. Habit
2. Desire for honor
3. Fear of punishment
4. Future happiness
5. Reverence for our Creator
6. Wealth
7. Power
8. Love |
| You could have the participants indicate their rating physically by standing on a line on the floor. | Urge the group members to rate each factor from one to ten as to the strength of its motivation for them.

Ask for volunteers to perform a role play. Give the following description to the volunteers: |
| This legend could be printed on newsprint or on a piece of paper. | "There is a Russian legend about the *Yurodivy*, which means 'born poor.' These are people in concentration camps who take on the punishment that is directed to others. The Yurodivy know that many persons, when they are punished by the guards, will return hate and thus multiply the evil in the world. The Yurodivy, how- |

Explanation and Adaptation	Program
	ever, take the violence and forgive, thus diminishing the content of the evil of the world."
	One character is to play a guard who is preparing to whip a prisoner. Another plays the victim. The third plays the Yurodivy.
Urge creativity here so that the play does not become cut-and-dried.	Urge them to use their imaginations. Give them time to talk together. While the volunteers prepare, tell the rest of the group that the role play will portray the Russian legend of the Yurodivy. Request the remaining participants to identify the feelings of each character. Have them search for the reasons for the behavior of each person.
	After the play, open the group discussion by reading the following quote from John Powell's *Unconditional Love* (Allen, Tex.: Argus Communications, 1978), p. 109:
	Saying "yes!" to God is not a simple matter because making our lives into lives of love is not a simple or easy thing. To choose love as a life principle means that my basic mindset or question must be: What is the loving thing to be, to do, to say? My consistent response to each of life's events, to each person who enters and touches my life, to each demand on my time and nerves and heart, must somehow be transformed into an act of love.
	Ask them how the role play relates to the quote. What was the motivation of the Yurodivy?
	E. *Historical Lovers of Christ* Throughout the centuries there have been many persons who have loved Christ and heroically served others because of that love. Tell the participants you are going to examine several of these individuals. Divide the group into four groups. Ask them to choose one of these persons (each group should select a different one):
	1. Elizabeth Garland Hall 2. Watchman Nee (Ni To-Sheng) 3. Dietrich Bonhoeffer 4. Martin Luther King, Jr.
An alternative would be to ask four persons to prepare ahead of time for their role. Then, using a talk-show format, the four might be interviewed by the group.	As the group members study the descriptive material of their person, they should focus on these questions: 1. What did the person accomplish? 2. Why did he (she) do it? 3. What did his (her) work cost him (her)?

Explanation and Adaptation	Program
	The group is to select one person who will portray the character in the following discussion. The group helps this person prepare.
Other historical characters could be selected. The persons should be ones with whom your particular group could especially identify. If others are selected, you would need to gather background information before the session.	1. **Elizabeth Garland Hall**, from Augusta, Maine, became an orphan at an early age when her parents died. Even though she had been told that her parents were from Europe near the Black Sea, she knew prejudice because of her dark skin. Elizabeth went to the Chicago Baptist Training School so that she could become a missionary. She married William A. Hall from Jamaica and became a missionary to Africa. After working hard serving the African people, Elizabeth got sick and had to return to the family home in Jamaica. She served the Jamaican people in many ways, including helping isolation patients during an epidemic and developing a home for little children. In the end, however, her health gave out and she returned to the United States and died shortly after her return.
	2. **Watchman Nee (Ni To-Sheng)** was born in 1903 in Foochow, China. This was a time of rebellion in China and during his early years, the Manchu Dynasty was swept away by revolution. During this same period of time another man was growing up, but he became influenced by Marxism and became a lifelong Communist. His name was Mao Tse-tung. Due to his mother's confession of Christianity, Watchman Nee became a strong force for Christ during a time in China when there was a strong anti-religion thrust.
	Nee took up the cause of Christ with dedication and enthusiasm. The prime motivation for his willingness to sacrifice can be found in his poem "Boundless Love."
	Thy love, broad, high, deep, endless, is truly without measure, for only so could such a sinner as I be thus abundantly blessed.
	My Lord paid a cruel price to buy me back and make me His. I can but carry His cross with gladness and follow Him steadfastly to the end.
	That's exactly what Nee did. He worked diligently to spread the gospel of Christ and was successful in making many converts. His sermons that were translated into English have made a great impact

Explanation and Adaptation	Program
	on persons outside China as well. Nee organized the "Little Flock" and enriched many lives through this fellowship. The communist government finally imprisoned Watchman Nee. Even during his imprisonment, he preached the gospel and made converts of the guards. He remained in prison for twenty years until his death in 1972. When the history of the Christian church in China is written, it will be impossible to ignore the life and work of Watchman Nee, whose influence will last and whose legacy is a Christian fellowship that survived the fires of persecution and the attempts to destroy the Christian church in China. 3. **Dietrich Bonhoeffer** was born in 1906 into a family of seven children in Breslau, in what is now East Germany. For him Christianity could never be merely intellectual theory, doctrine divorced from life, or mystical emotion. Instead, it had to be responsible, obedient action—the discipleship of Christ—in every situation of everyday life, both private and public. It was this viewpoint that led him to prison and death in the end. Bonhoeffer studied in Tübingen and Berlin and finally received his doctorate in theology in 1927. His first position was as curate under a parish priest at the German Lutheran Community in Barcelona, Spain, and he gave himself wholeheartedly to the task. When Bonhoeffer returned to Germany, the Nazis were beginning to take over the government. He became a professor at the university and began to oppose the Nazis, especially Hitler's leadership. His views were disliked by the Nazis, and they cut off one of his lecture broadcasts on the radio. Shortly after this he left for England to pastor two German congregations there. While preparing to visit Gandhi in India, he received a call from the "Confessing Church" in Germany (those churches opposed to Hitler) to take charge of an illegal, clandestine seminary in Pomerania. He decided to accept this call and take over the proposed responsibilities, but the Nazis soon closed the school and forbade him even to write. It was at this time that he got involved with his sister, her husband, and General Fritsch in planning to overthrow Hitler. In April, 1943, he was arrested and

Explanation and Adaptation	Program
	imprisoned. At the time of his arrest, Bonhoeffer said, "When Christ calls a man, he bids him come and die." Shortly before the Allies invaded Germany on April 8, 1945, Dietrich Bonhoeffer was executed. 4. **Martin Luther King, Jr.** (1929–1968) was raised in Atlanta, Georgia. He was the son of a preacher, and he accepted Christ during a revival when he was five-and-a-half years old. From that day forward, Martin sought to live his faith in his home and his community. That was not an easy thing during the days of his childhood. Blacks were cruelly separated from the benefits enjoyed by the whites. He was disillusioned by the behavior of white Christians and yearned for a society of equality. Martin pursued his education at Morehouse College, Crozer Theological Seminary, and Boston College Graduate School. His studies brought him closer to God, and he came to understand how Christians could use their faith to be witnesses of God's love—not only for individuals but for all people. Mahatma Gandhi had a great influence on Martin. From Gandhi, he learned that true pacifism was not nonresistance to evil; true pacifism was *nonviolent resistance* to evil. This view helped lead him to a nonviolent crusade for civil rights for all people. Martin Luther King, Jr., led the Montgomery bus boycott and founded the Southern Christian Leadership Conference. He led many protest marches and sit-ins. Through his efforts and the efforts of others, the Civil Rights Act of 1964 became law. He was jailed several times and publicly derided by many. Martin continued his struggle to seek civil rights for all until he was assassinated in Memphis, Tennessee, in 1968. • • • • Gather the total group again. Each person selected to portray a character is now interviewed by members of the other groups. After the interviews are over, ask the group to discuss the following questions: 1. What are the similarities of these persons? 2. What makes each one different? F. *In-Depth Bible Encounter* Have the group count off by twos. Assign Matthew 16:24-26 to those whose number is one and Romans

Explanation and Adaptation	Program
	12:1-2 to those whose number is two. Tell them that each person is to write an original paraphrase of the assigned passage. They are not to use the words from their text and should try to keep the length of the paraphrase about the same as the original. After writing the paraphrase, the participants are to ponder the question "What would happen if we took this passage seriously?" Now ask the participants to form a group with the other persons who worked on the same passage (all of the ones in one group and all of the twos in the other). They are to share their paraphrases and what they feel would happen if they took the passage seriously.
	Request the participants to reassemble. Each group should select one person to share some of the learnings from the group. Then summarize the learnings from the study.
	G. *Cross Bearing for One Another* Place the wood pieces in the middle of the group. Tell the group that to love God through Christ is to be willing to carry our own crosses. It also means that we are willing to help others bear their crosses.
This exercise should not be mandatory; however, the leader should present the idea convincingly so that each person will want to take part. Have them carry the piece of wood with them at all times.	The pieces of wood are symbolic of pieces of Christ's cross. They are also to symbolize the crosses of members of the group. Ask the participants to share pressures that they feel they are carrying that are causing them difficulty. Urge someone else in the group to be willing to help carry that pressure during the next week. Once someone assumes the cross, the person with the pressure selects a piece of wood to give to the other person. The one carrying the "cross" piece is to pray for the other person and make time during the week to share with her or him.
You may want to follow up on this exercise next week.	Urge each participant to share a pressure and share someone else's cross. Some persons might want to take more than one cross piece.
If you don't like the group hug, hold hands or just stand in a circle. If this session is held in the evening, the closing may be held by candlelight.	H. *Closing—Prayer of Commission* Gather the group into a group hug for prayer. Ask each person to pray for someone else. The prayers should be supportive and loving. The leader will close the prayer with a commissioning statement. The prayer should emphasize that because Christ loved us first by giving his life on the cross, we can love others by helping to carry their crosses. Ask for the Holy Spirit's guidance to each person.

The Cross and Suffering

Don Harrington

Explanation and Adaptation	Program
The focus of this session is to help the participants feel a connection with Christ.	Objectives: • To help participants identify with Christ's ability to endure the pain and suffering of the cross. • To enable participants to explore the pain and suffering that they experience. • To help participants recognize the power that Christ can give to help us cope with pain and suffering.
This session can be lengthened or shortened by adjusting the activities.	Overview of the Session: A. Getting Started B. Examining Christ's Suffering C. Letter Simulation D. Bible Discovery—The Last Seven Words E. Grab-Bag Response F. Celebration G. Closing
Prepare the newsprint, slips of paper, and letters ahead of time.	Resources and Materials Needed: Bibles, paper (white and multicolored), scissors, glue, pencils, posterboard, markers, envelope(s), and a bowl. The Session in Detail: A. *Getting Started* Print the name of each participant on a piece of paper. Place the paper slips in a box. Have each person choose another person's name by drawing it out of the box. If someone draws his or her own name, have her or him replace the slip and draw again.
Print the situations on newsprint. Post it on the wall so that each person can make a selection.	Have the participants, one at a time, describe how this person would react to one of the following situations: 1. He (or she) learns that his (or her) father or mother was in a severe accident.

Explanation and Adaptation	Program
These situations may be difficult for younger youth to respond to. Substitute others as necessary. Please keep the theme, however. An alternative would be to use the names or entertainers or sports stars instead of persons in the group. This alternative might work especially well with younger youth.	2. He (or she) is injured in a swimming accident and becomes paralyzed from the neck down. 3. He (or she) learns that his (or her) home had caught on fire and burned to the ground. After the reactions are described, the rest of the group is to guess who this person is. Have participants choose a partner and share several things that have brought them pain in the last few months. How has this pain made them feel?
List responses on newsprint.	B. *Examining Christ's Suffering* Display either a crucifix (a cross on which there is a figure representing Christ) or a picture of a crucifix. Ask the participants, "When you see a crucifix, what do you think about?" Summarize their comments. Try to communicate the idea that a crucifix helps people recall Christ's suffering. Tell the group that you are now going to examine the events surrounding the cross so that everyone may closely investigate Christ's suffering, both physical and psychological. Begin by dividing the participants into four groups. Assign a different passage to each group.
Have questions on newsprint.	1. Matthew 27:15-56 2. Mark 15:6-41 3. Luke 23:6-49 4. John 18:38–19:37 As the groups study their passages, have them answer these questions: • What kinds of pain did Jesus suffer in his last hours? (Try to look for more than physical pain.) • What was the source of the pain? • What are some other ways in which Jesus could have responded? Ask the groups to record their discoveries on newsprint. Once the groups have completed their lists, have them reassemble as a total group. Ask each group to report its findings. Compare the lists to identify similarities and differences. Try to discover the uniqueness of each Gospel account.
If this exercise seems too heavy for your group, get a copy of Billy Joel's	C. *Letter Simulation* This next activity must be entered into with sensitivity

Explanation and Adaptation	Program
rock-and-roll song "You're Only Human." Use the same reflection questions after listening to it. If you do use this exercise, please be sensitive to your young people. You may have to follow up the session with private conversations.	and compassion. Do it with the whole group unless there are several adult counselors. Each one could do the exercise in a smaller group. Print the following letter and place it in an envelope. (Make multiple copies if there will be more than one group.) Explain to the group members that this is only a simulation. Have someone read the letter aloud, treating it as if it came from one of the members. Ask them to listen carefully to the pain that this young person is feeling.
This letter is a compilation of actual suicide notes.	Friends, By the time you read this letter I will be gone. I have thought about this for a long time and have decided that I can't stand the pain any longer. Each day causes me no end of sorrow. Every morning when I get up and look in the mirror I wonder why God would make someone so ugly. None of my friends ever have to suffer because of their looks. Why do I? My biggest disappointment is that I never could live up to the expectations of my parents. My mother wanted me to be popular. My dad was never satisfied with my grades at school. I wish I could have done something to make them satisfied with me. When I go to school, the pain continues when I have to hear the rumors and gossip spread about me. Half of it is so distorted, it doesn't even make sense. Why do people talk about other people? I have finally discovered that death has to be better than this living. Please remember me. Good-bye. Dawn
Some youth may know persons who have attempted or committed suicide. The discussion might need to be followed up with a session on suicide prevention.	Discuss the contents of the letter. What were the things that hurt Dawn? Have you ever had these same feelings? What other pains do friends your age have?
	D. *Bible Discovery—The Seven Last Words* Assign a different statement to each person or group of persons. If there are fewer than seven in your group, assign multiple passages. Have them read the passage in more than one translation. What do these statements reveal about how we can—because of the cross—handle human suffering?

Explanation and Adaptation	Program
You may have to give assistance to some of these groups to discover the redemptive aspect of the passage. It may be helpful for your group to work on one passage together before moving into smaller groups.	1. The prayer for Christ's enemies—Luke 23:34 2. The promise to the repentant robber—Luke 23:43 3. The charges to the mother of Jesus and to the beloved disciple—John 19:26, 27 4. The cry of desolation—Mark 15:34; Matthew 27:46 5. The cry of physical anguish—John 19:28 6. The cry of victory—John 19:30 7. The cry of surrender—Luke 23:46
	Have the persons or groups share their discoveries. If a person can't find the learning in the passage, let the rest of the group help. In Matthew 26:42 Jesus described the cross experience as a "cup of suffering" that he must drink. Did Jesus resign or surrender himself to the impending suffering? What difference does it make?
On newsprint, print a dictionary definition of the two words "resignation" and "surrender" or use whatever words would communicate this general message.	Conclude this section with this statement: "The resurrection of Jesus Christ is God's evidence that what happened on the cross was finished, accepted, and triumphant. We must always look at the cross from the vantage point of the empty tomb. Together, the tree and the tomb say to us, 'Your suffering is not in vain!'"
	E. *Grab-Bag Response* Divide the group into four small groups. Print the following situations of suffering on a piece of paper and place them in a container. Have each group select one.
Encourage the groups to identify a number of possible options. They might want to develop endings for their story based on the different options.	Before they read the situation, ask them to decide how they would share with a friend who had the experience described. Have them keep in mind Christ's experience on the cross.
	• **Tina** had dreamed for years of finding a special boyfriend. When she thought she had found him, she threw herself totally into the relationship. Then, suddenly, she discovered that she was pregnant. Her boyfriend told her that he loved her but didn't want a baby or marriage. He demanded that if she didn't get an abortion, he would leave her. She refused and he abandoned her.
	• **Barry** used to live in an upper-middle-class neighborhood. His family had a fine home and some beautiful cars. Last year, however, his father was arrested, tried, and convicted for embezzlement of company funds. He is now serving a prison sentence in the

Explanation and Adaptation	Program
	state penitentiary. His family's possessions have been repossessed. Barry and his mother have moved into an apartment. He has received much ridicule from his friends and others.
	• **Lynelle** was a free spirit who loved people, sports, and the outdoors. One afternoon she was in the park meditating. She was deep in her thoughts when a man came along and hit her in the head. After falling to the ground stunned from the blow, she could feel the man remove her clothes. The rest was just a blur to her, but she knew that she had been personally violated. She has never been the same since that time.
	• **Tracy** wakes up and experiences severe pain. He realizes that he is in the hospital with multiple broken bones. His memory is vague, but soon his thoughts go back to the night before. Almost all of his friends were there; what a party it was! Everyone was drunk including him. Then he remembers that he left the party with two of those friends. He asks the nurse about them. She hesitates and then tells him that they died during the night. One of those friends was his girlfriend, whom he had known and loved since he was very young. The other friend was his buddy, with whom he had shared many ups and downs. How could he face tomorrow?
	Bring the groups back together after they have had time to formulate their responses. Let them share the situation and their response. Encourage interaction.
	F. *Celebration* Hand out multicolored slips of paper to the participants. Try to give a different color to each person if possible.
Make a label for the bowl. Print the phrase "The Arms of God."	Ask each person to write down a pain that they are presently suffering. If they are experiencing several, have them record the one that hurts the most. To symbolize their giving these pains to God, urge them to tear the slip of paper into small pieces and place these into the bowl. (The pieces should be small enough not to leave any pain visible.)
A facsimile could already have been made so that it might be traced.	Each person should now cut a cross-shaped bookmark out of the posterboard. One side of the bookmark is to be covered with some of the pieces from the bowl. Glue the pieces onto the bookmark.

Explanation and Adaptation	**Program**
	Explain to the group that we are the body of Christ. As Christ's body we have a responsibility to support others. The bookmark will be a reminder of our connection with our friends' pains.
	G. *Closing* Christ suffered on the cross for each one of us. Christ's victory over the cross shows us that we can have power over our suffering. Draw the participants together in a circle. Allow time for each person to share a *sentence* that communicates what they have learned. Urge them to pray brief prayers for one another. The leader should close the prayer.

A Nation of Priests

Alonza Lawrence

Explanation and Adaptation	Program
	Objective: • To help participants understand the position of priest and how we all function as priests in the church today. **Overview of the Session:** A. Getting Started B. Searching the Scriptures C. Me, a Mediator? D. Reflections on Personal Priesthood. E. Construction of Vestments F. Closing—Commission Service. **Materials Needed:** Bibles, journals, construction paper in a variety of colors, newsprint, markers, at least one good reference Bible with dictionary, flashlight, at least two blankets, index cards, materials to make vestments.
Encourage the group to think beyond the clergy persons in your own church.	**The Session in Detail:** A. *Getting Started* Ask the group to reflect on persons that they have seen or met who act in the role of priests or ministers. They may recall personal experiences, movies, stories, or any information that they have come in contact with. Now ask them to separate the personalities and the functions of the individuals. List on newsprint the functions or services these people provide. Discuss them briefly in broad, general terms. B. *Search the Scriptures* Divide the group into clusters of three to five persons. Assign each cluster one of the following Scriptures

Explanation and Adaptation	Program
	with the task of answering the question beside it. Ask the clusters to choose one person to report their findings.

Leaders will want to be familiar with these passages in order to assist the group in defining terms used.

- Deuteronomy 33:8-10—What is the job of the priest?
- Exodus 19:5-6—Who does God desire to be priest?
- Leviticus 16:20-22—What is the symbolic meaning of this ceremony and what part does the priest play?

Reconvene the total group and ask the clusters to report. Have them read their Scriptures and answer the questions assigned. Discuss each answer in the large group and pull from the group answers to the following questions, "Who are priests?" "What do priests do?" and "What is the meaning of the terms 'mediator' and 'teacher'?"

Look again at the list of services. Are there similarities in the functions listed and what the group is now discovering?

C. *Me, a Mediator?*

Read to the group Leviticus 16:11-14. Explain about the innermost chamber (the "Holy of Holies") of the temple. Only the high priest could go in once a year for the Day of Atonement, and only after cleansing himself in special ceremonies.

The Holy of Holies was considered the most sacred of all places. This chamber housed the Ark of the Covenant guarded by two cherubim, signifying the presence of God.

With chairs and blankets construct a "Holy of Holies." Have one person serve as priest and have the rest of the group act as members of the tribe. Have the members of the tribe write out requests to be offered by the priest in the "Holy of Holies." The name of the individual making the request must be on the request. The priest will collect the written requests and enter the "Holy of Holies." Make sure that the tribe cannot see the priest. There will need to be a flashlight and marker in the "Holy of Holies" before the priest enters.

Do not inform the tribe of what will happen. While under the blankets the priest will randomly write yes or no on each request. After a few minutes the priest will come out and return the requests. Ask the group to remain quiet while this is happening.

Now discuss how the group felt in their roles, how the priest felt in making the decisions, and how the tribe members felt when their requests were returned. Also discuss the feeling of having someone mediate for them when they make requests.

Explanation and Adaptation	Program
	Divide the group in half, giving Hebrews 10:5-25 to one and Jeremiah 31:31-34 to the other. Ask each group to read its passage and compare it to the Leviticus passage. What differences do they see? Why are those differences important? Ask the total group to share their findings. On newsprint list the differences as they are described. D. *Reflections on Personal Priesthood* In their journals or on pieces of paper have members of the group reflect on their relationship with God. What does it mean to be a priest or a minister? Would other people sometimes say to them, "You function as a priest or a minister"? This reflection is for their own use and is not to be shared with the group at large.
You might want to capture these ideas on newsprint to use in the closing of this session.	After allowing time for writing, ask each person to join with two other persons to make groups of three. Ask each group to think of a situation either at church, in your community, or at school that needs someone to function as minister or priest. When they have thought of a situation, list ways that they can minister in that place. Bring all the groups together for a time of sharing.
You might find it helpful to have pictures of clergy vestments to give an idea to the group. If time is a factor you might suggest that the group merely make clerical collars.	E. *Construction of Vestments* Ministers or priests wear a variety of vestments, such as robes, collars, stoles, and so on. Have a variety of materials available and ask each person to create a vestment to wear for the rest of the day. F. *Closing—Commission Service* As the first step in the closing, ask group members to look again at the list made at the beginning of the session of the functions of priests or ministers. Have them write on an index card several of those functions that they perform in their lives. After everyone has made a list, have the group gather in a circle. Begin with words similar to these: "Today we have been looking at what it means to be a minister or a priest. We learned that under the Old Covenant the priest served as a mediator between the people and God. But in the New Covenant we are all priests and we need no one to be a mediator between ourselves and God. As priests or ministers we have the responsibility to serve one another. As a part of our closing today we will commission one another to go out and be ministers or priests to the world."

Explanation and Adaptation	**Program**
	Have someone read 1 Peter 2:9-10 slowly and clearly. If you have a variety of translations available, you might have several persons read from different translations.
	After the reading, say words similar to these: "We are a royal priesthood; we are God's people. We go forth to share our gifts with others. I invite you to share your gifts for ministry with us now and with the world when you leave." At this point pause so that each person can share the gifts written on his or her card. After each person has spoken, the group should respond, "_____, you are a minister; share your gifts with the world."
Have the chant on newsprint where it can be seen by all. Do the cheer three times, increasing the group's volume each time.	When all have shared, close with a cheer: Once we were no people, But now we are God's people. Once we had not received mercy, But now we have received mercy. Once we had no gifts, But now we have many gifts. We are the people of God. We are God's ministers to the world. Amen! Amen! Amen!

Mission Is Sending
Steve Youd

Explanation and Adaptation	Program
Please do not share the objective printed here at the start of the session. You will be sharing the objective at the conclusion of the "Getting Started" exercise.	**Objective:** To help participants understand mission as a *sending* enterprise in which a perfect God enlists imperfect persons for particular tasks. **Overview of the Session:** 　A. Getting Started—"Life's Most Embarrassing Photos" 　B. Search the Scriptures—A Letter to Moses 　C. The Call to Mission 　　1. A look at Isaiah (perceiving a mission) 　　2. A look at Adoniram Judson (preparing for mission) 　D. Reflective Meditation—"We Are the World." 　E. Closing—A Narrow Prayer to a Wide God **Resources and Materials Needed:** "Life's most embarrassing photos" (brought by young people), Bibles, writing paper, writing utensils, newsprint, markers, masking tape, record or tape of "We Are the World," record or tape player. **The Session in Detail:** A. *Getting Started—"Life's Most Embarrassing Photos"* Instruct the young people to take out the picture they brought of themselves. One by one, have the young people share why they find the picture so embarrassing (for example: "It shows my fat legs," "My braces take up the whole picture," "My hair looks as if I had put my finger in an electrical socket," etc.). You may want to do yours first to demonstrate what you mean. Instruct those who do not have photos to think of what
A couple of weeks prior to this session, begin publicizing to the young people that they will be needing to bring in a photograph of themselves which they find to be less than flattering. It can be a recent or not-so-recent picture. It can be funny or serious. But, it should be a picture that they (for whatever reason) *honestly* find embarrassing.	

Explanation and Adaptation	Program
	they would do if they were granted one wish to change one thing about themselves (height, weight, nose structure, etc.).
	After the entire group has had an opportunity to share, point out the following: 1. Everyone wants to be seen in the best possible light. 2. We all have certain things we perceive as "imperfections." 3. God chooses imperfect people to do the work of the gospel.
Whenever a section is written in quotation marks, it can be used as a minilecture.	B. *Search the Scriptures—A Letter to Moses* "Today we are going to be looking at the word 'mission.' Can anyone tell me what the word 'mission' means? [Take suggestions.] The term 'mission' comes to us from the Latin 'missio' which means 'to send.' For our purposes here, we will define mission as a *sending* enterprise in which a perfect God enlists imperfect persons for particular tasks. Let's read a portion of Scripture together in which we find God calling a great person—a great, *imperfect* person. It is the story of the calling of Moses."
It may be fun to have a few different readers here (the narrator, God, Moses).	As a group, read Exodus 3:10-12; 4:10-13. Then, give the following instructions: "At this point I am going to ask each of you to write a letter to Moses. In it I want you to include at least the following:
It is best to have these categories already printed and run off so that each person can have an individual copy to use to draft a letter, or have them written on newsprint and have the group copy them on sheets of paper.	• how you perceive that Moses was thinking about himself; • why you think Moses was feeling the way he did; • whether you think Moses was feeling better or worse by the end of the conversation with God; • how Moses' image of himself compared with the way God saw him; • how you would have felt in the situation; • an instance when you felt like Moses; • how you think God feels about you; • whether you see yourself as you think God sees you.
Have each young person go off to an isolated spot to ensure that it will be an *individual* undertaking. Wander around to answer questions and to get a feeling for the progress people are making.	"Try to include all of this in an actual letter format, just as though you were writing to a friend. I'll give you as much time as you need. Do a good job. We'll be sharing the letters when you finish."
If your group is a large one (more	Reconvene the group. Ask for volunteers to share their letters. If time (and/or embarrassment) is an issue, everyone need not share in the total-group setting.

Explanation and Adaptation	Program

Explanation and Adaptation

than fifteen participants), you may want to break into small groups to read the letters. The total group can reconvene after the small groups have finished, with a few volunteers sharing their letters.

Have the newsprint and markers ready and available to be taken by a representative from each group.

As this may be a difficult assignment for teenagers, be certain to do a bit of "roaming" to offer suggestions and encouragement.

An alternative would be to use another person here such as Lulu Fleming, Helen Barrett Montgomery, or a person from your congregation who has been involved in the community. Have the four reasons already printed on a piece of newsprint and ready for hanging. If your group is interested in learning more about Adoniram Judson, the brochure "Adoniram Judson: God's Catalyst" is available. Copies can be secured by writing: The Board of International Ministries, American Baptist Churches, USA, P.O. Box 851, Valley Forge, PA 19482-0851.

Program

C. *The Call to Mission*
   1. A look at Isaiah (perceiving a mission)
      "So far, we have seen that our God, a perfect God, enlists imperfect people to do the divine will. I want you now, in groups of three, to look at a potential missionary: Isaiah. You are going to be reading Isaiah 6:1-8.

      "After reading the passage, your group is to imagine that God is going to send the three of you, like Isaiah, off to a mission field. Your assignment is to list on newsprint as many things as you can possibly think of in two categories:

      • things you can do to prepare to be a good missionary *before* you go to your new mission area,
      • things you can do to be a good missionary *after* you have arrived at your new mission field.

"Appoint a spokesperson from your group who will hang your piece of newsprint and explain it. Time is limited, so work quickly."

Reconvene the group. Have each spokesperson hang his or her group's piece of newsprint and explain it.

   2. A look at Adoniram Judson (preparing for mission)
      "Your strategies for the preparation and adaptation to mission were excellent. Before we close, let me hang one last piece of newsprint. It is about one of the 'giants' of the mission field and why he was so effective. His name was Adoniram Judson. He was the person largely responsible for bringing into being the very first Protestant foreign mission society in all of America. People say he was effective for at least four reasons:

      • He mastered the foreign language he would be speaking;
      • He adapted his living to the culture;
      • He developed priorities for ministry;
      • He never lost sight of his evangelistic goal even though he worked for six years before seeing results.

      "Adoniram Judson was a great missionary, but he was not perfect. Like Moses and Isaiah (or any other believer, for that matter) he was an imperfect person who listened to the voice of a perfect God."

Explanation and Adaptation	**Program**
If you cannot secure the record or tape, simply read the words of the chorus while the young people's eyes are closed.	D. *Reflective Meditation—"We Are the World."* "In our day, there are some imperfect people who have heard the voice of a perfect God. They have heard God calling them to remember those less fortunate than themselves. I want you to close your eyes and listen to the words of the music I am about to play. During this record, you may want to say, like Isaiah, 'Here am I, send me.'"
Perhaps some in the group will know the words of the chorus and can print them on newsprint for the group.	Play record or tape of "We Are the World," by Lionel Richie and Michael Jackson. After the time of reflection, allow time for the group to share their thoughts. Provide an opportunity for anyone who feels led to make a new commitment.
Go directly into this prayer at the conclusion of "We Are the World."	E. *Closing—A Narrow Prayer to a Wide God* Oh, Lord, you are such a wide God and I am such a narrow person. Help me, help us to see a little wider, to feel a little wider, to understand a little wider, to entertain wider thoughts, even the thought "Here am I; send me." Amen.

Mission Is Serving

Steve Youd

Explanation and Adaptation	Program

Please do not share the objective printed here at the start of the session. You will be sharing the objectives at the conclusion of the "Getting Started" exercise.	Objective:
	• To help participants understand mission as a *serving* enterprise in which *all* Christians are ministers.
	
	Overview of the Session:
	  A. Getting Started—"Who Recognizes the Minister?"
	  B. Search the Scriptures—"Out of Service"
	  C. The Call to Ministry
	    1. A look at "building the cross" (horizontal and vertical)
	    2. A look at "picking up the cross" (case studies)
	  D. Reflective Meditation—"I Have a Dream."
	  E. Closing—A Prayer to See Without Seeing
	
	Resources and Materials Needed:
	One religious periodical (with pictorials), Bible, writing utensils, newsprint, markers, masking tape, six Scripture verses written on 8½-by-11-inch paper, recording of "I Have a Dream" speech.
	
	The Session in Detail:

Be certain that whatever religious periodical you use, it has many photographs of people. There should be persons who are young and old; male and female; black, white, Hispanic, and Asian.	A. *Getting Started—"Who Recognizes the Minister?"* Hold up a religious periodical in front of your teenagers. Tell them that in the periodical there are pictures of some ministers. You will flip through the periodical, and they are to shout, "Stop!" when they have spotted a person they think is a minister. Place an "X" by any pictures where the young people instruct you to stop. When you have finished flipping through the periodical, explain that you will tell the young people in a moment how well they did in identifying ministers. If your group has done Session 16 in this book, you

Explanation and Adaptation	**Program**
	might begin by tying in that work with today's focus. If your group has not done Session 16, you might begin by saying that mission has been defined as "a *sending* enterprise in which a perfect God enlists imperfect persons for particular tasks." Then continue as given in the session plan. Stating the following may be appropriate:
When a section is enclosed in quotation marks, it can be used as a mini-lecture. Be certain to affirm any serious answers, even if they are not exactly what you are looking for.	"In our last session we defined the term 'mission.' Can anyone remember how we defined it? [Take suggestions.] Our exact definition was 'a *sending* enterprise in which a perfect God enlists imperfect persons for particular tasks.' Today we are going to be looking at the word 'ministry.' Can anyone tell me what the word 'ministry' means? [Take suggestions.] In the Bible, the word 'ministry' is most often interpreted as *service*. So, when we talk of 'mission as ministry,' we are realizing that God *sends* people to *serve*. Speaking realistically, you cannot talk of 'mission' without also talking of 'ministry.' And you cannot talk of 'ministry' without also talking of 'mission.' *Sending* and *serving* go hand in hand."
Do not attempt to elicit a serious answer out of this first question.	At this point, take the following poll of the young people: • How many of you view yourselves as imperfect people? • How many of you believe that God can and does use imperfect people? • How many of you have ever served someone else (i.e., ever performed an act of kindness for someone else)? Follow the poll by explaining that what they have told you is that they are all ministers—that God uses each and every one of them to serve others. That is what being a minister is!
It is necessary to repeat the question only long enough to drive home the point that all believers are ministers.	Now return to the periodical. Flip through the periodical once again, continually asking the question "Is that person a minister?" as you point to the various photographs. If they understand, you will receive an affirmative answer at each juncture.
	B. *Search the Scriptures—"Out of Service"* "Now that we know that ministering means serving, let's seek to identify who it is that needs our service. Perhaps we can best do this by looking at who Jesus identified for service."

Explanation and Adaptation	Program
	As a group read Luke 4:16-21. Then, break into four small groups. Give each small group a piece of newsprint and a felt-tip marker, assigning each group one of the questions that follow. Each group should appoint a "scribe" (who will write the group's answers on newsprint) and "spokesperson" (who will subsequently interpret the small group's answers to the total group). 1. How are people *poor* today? 2. How are people *captive* today? 3. How are people *oppressed* today? 4. How are people *blind* today?
Some of the groups will probably come up with similar answers even though they are exploring different terms. This is to be expected and is perfectly acceptable.	When each group has filled its newsprint with responses to its particular question, reconvene the group. Each spokesperson can now come forward, tape the newsprint in an appropriate location, and explain the group's observations.
	C. *The Call to Ministry* 1. A look at "building the cross" (horizontal and vertical) "Jesus asks us to 'pick up your cross and follow me' (Matthew 16:24). A cross has two parts: a vertical and a horizontal. The ministry to which Jesus calls us also has two parts. The first, the vertical, reminds us of the need to establish a relationship with God. The second, the horizontal, reminds us of the need to establish a relationship with humanity. We must keep both in mind as we seek to minister. In his book *Christian Mission in the Modern World* (Downer's Grove, Ill: Inter-Varsity Press, 1976), John R. Stott has stated, 'Our neighbor is neither a bodiless soul that we should love only his soul, nor a soulless body that we should care for its welfare alone.' We must care for the spiritual *and* the physical needs of those to whom we seek to minister." At this juncture, tell the group that they will be helping you put together a cross. You will be reading to them six verses of Scripture, and they must decide whether the verse represents a horizontal element or vertical element of the cross. One of the verses symbolizes the intersection of the two. As a consensus is reached, use masking tape to hang these Scriptures in an appropriate location.
Have these Scriptures printed on sheets of typing paper prior to the start of the session.	Matthew 25:34-40 (horizontal) Mark 12:30-31 (intersection) Luke 12:32 (vertical)

Explanation and Adaptation	Program
	John 5:24 (vertical) 2 Corinthians 5:18 (vertical) James 2:15-16 (horizontal) 2. A look at "picking up the cross" (case studies) Below are three actual case studies. Only names have been changed. Divide your young people into three groups. Assign a case study to each group and tell them that they are to determine how best to minister in the given situation. Each group should select a "scribe" (to document on newsprint the group's ideas), a "reader" (to read the case study to the total group when it reconvenes), and a "spokesperson" (to explain the small group's response to its case study).
We hope that in their responses, the young people will: 1. Take the girl's threat seriously. 2. Ask the girl some important questions: "Have you ever thought of killing yourself before?" "How often do you think about it?" "Have you ever tried?" 3. Put the girl in touch with someone who can provide professional guidance. Any response should include, *at least* encouraging the girl to take the information to an adult she can trust so that the family problem can be addressed and the abuser confronted.	**Case Study #1**—Dumped by Her Boyfriend A female friend of yours has recently been "dumped" by her boyfriend in favor of a new girl. Weeks later, your friend is still struggling with the rejection. During this time, you received the following note from her: "It is hard for me to go to Teens and to see him with Frannie .... My only solution to the whole thing is to drop out ... then kill myself, because then I will be able to forget about him and make him and Fran happy, and make my family happy, because I don't think anybody will miss me." How do you minister (serve) in this situation? **Case Study #2**—Trouble with Father You've just been to a youth retreat. The topic? Sexuality. At the retreat no doors were left unopened. Participants talked about premarital sex, masturbation, birth control, incest, fantasy, and so on. As you are heading back to the church, there is one other passenger in your car: a seventeen-year-old girl. She is very quiet and seems to be disturbed about something. Suddenly she asks a question: "Have you ever talked to anyone about incest?" You answer, "Not really. Why do you ask?" There is a long pause. The girl, through her sobs, says, "I've never told anyone this before, but my father has forced me to sleep with him." How do you minister (serve) in this situation?
It is hoped that the young people might come up with such responses as: 1. It's okay to question. 2. At various times, God says "Yes," "No," or "Wait!"	**Case Study #3**—Doubts About God Tom is away at college. A track star in high school, he had been training hard and doing well at the university—until the injury to his knee. In his latest letter, he writes, "The doctor diagnosed my problem as patella tendinitis. Of course his first advice was to stop

Explanation and Adaptation	Program
3. It doesn't appear to be God's will to heal everyone (for example, the apostle Paul's thorn in the flesh). 4. It does appear that God wants us to learn through our adversities.	running. So I did; I didn't run at all from late December, through January, and up until now. I can't begin to tell you how terribly frustrating, depressing, and hard to take this is. It hits me in my heart, right at the thing that I love to do. I've read lots of Scripture about how God hears and is concerned about all our problems and how God loves us and wants the very best for us. I've read about how 'The prayer of faith shall save the sick.' I read how we ought to pray about such things and seek God's help in time of need. I pray and pray every day, but receive no answers and see no progress." How do you minister (serve) in this situation? When each group has had a chance to determine an approach to its case study, reconvene the total group. Have each group's "speaker" read the case study prior to having the "spokesperson" hang and explain its newsprinted responses.
	D. *Reflective Meditation—"I Have a Dream."* "Today, we have been talking about the term 'ministry'—service. One Baptist pastor knew well the meaning of the word 'ministry'—Dr. Martin Luther King, Jr. Dr. King was effective because he could envision the world being different. The Bible says that 'Where there is no vision, the people perish' (Proverbs 29:18). In August 1963, Dr. King, on the steps of the Lincoln Memorial, shared a part of his vision for ministry. "Now take a moment to get comfortable, to close your eyes and to listen to one man's vision."
If you have the record or tape, more of the speech could be shared.	Read or play the excerpt from Dr. King's "I Have a Dream" speech. . . . even though we must face the difficulties of today and tomorrow, I still have a dream. It is a dream deeply rooted in the American dream that one day this nation will rise up and live out the true meaning of its creed. We hold these truths to be self-evident, that all men are created equal. I have a dream that one day on the red hills of Georgia sons of former slaves and sons of former slave-owners will be able to sit down together at the table of brotherhood. I have a dream my four little children will one day live in a nation where they will not be judged by the color of their skin, but by the content of their character. . . .

Explanation and Adaptation	Program
	I have a dream that one day every valley shall be exalted, every hill and mountain shall be made low, the rough places shall be made plain, and the crooked places shall be made straight and the glory of the Lord shall be revealed and all flesh shall see it together.
	This is our hope. This is the faith that I go back to the South with.
	With this faith we will be able to hew out of the mountain of despair a stone of hope. . . .
	After listening, ask the group to share their thoughts/feelings about the speech. Now ask them to think about their dream or vision for the world, what they are willing to work toward. If possible, ask group members to write the vision down so it can be shared with others.
A suggestion for a valuable resource: If your group is interested in some truly innovative avenues for ministry, an excellent resource is available. Entitled *The Catalog of Creative Ministries*, by Virgil and Lynn Nelson (Valley Forge: Judson Press, 1983), this book highlights more than three hundred fresh ideas for hands-on ministry.	E. *Closing—A Prayer to See Without Seeing* As a total group, gather in a circle for a time of closing. Ask those who are willing to do so to share their vision or dream with the group. After each sharing, have the group respond, "You can do it with God's help." When all have had the opportunity to share, close with the following prayer. O Lord, help us to see without actually seeing, to hear without actually hearing, to feel without actually feeling. Grant, O God, that we might dream and then seek to live out our dream, for Christ's sake. Amen.

Freedom: What Is It?

Elizabeth J. Loughhead

Explanation and Adaptation	Program

When young people think of religion or the church, they usually do not think of freedom. More often they think of rules, restraints, and restrictions.	**Objective:**
	• To help members of the group understand freedom as it is defined by our heritage and tradition as Christians and as American Baptists.
	
	Overview of the Session:
	  A. Getting Started
	  B. Studying the Scriptures
	  C. Discovering the Baptist Tradition
	  D. Making It Personal
	  E. Closing
	
	Resources and Materials Needed:
	  Pictures or signs, newsprint and markers or chalkboard and chalk, Bibles, paper and pencils.
	
	The Session in Detail:
	
	A. *Getting Started*
	  Freedom is something that is often taken for granted by those of us who live in the United States. It may be a theoretical concept expressed in the Bill of Rights or the Preamble to the Constitution. It may be defined merely in political terms. Often we think of freedom only when we celebrate a national holiday such as the Fourth of July or Martin Luther King's birthday, or when we feel that our personal freedom has been infringed upon. This session will help you think about freedom in a different way. You may call it theological thinking because you will see what the Bible says about freedom and will discover that true freedom is found in Jesus Christ.

These comments are for the leader and need not be shared with the whole group.	

Explanation and Adaptation	Program
	To help the group begin to define freedom and to determine how it is valued by them, begin with an auction.
The money used can be play money from a "Monopoly" set or other game. Or each person can be given a slip of paper with an amount written on it. As he or she "buys" something, the amount spent is subtracted from the beginning total. Each person begins with the same amount.	On newsprint or the chalkboard write a list of what will be auctioned. Give each person some "money" with which to bid and buy. Each player begins with the same amount.
	To be auctioned are: friendship love truth popularity faith freedom health responsibility success
	The auctioneer names each word in turn and sells it to the highest bidder.
	The group should then discuss the bidding. • Which item was sold for the most money? • How much did freedom sell for? • What does this say about how highly freedom is valued?
If it is difficult to find pictures, write the words or phrases on 8½-by-11-inch sheets of paper and post them on the walls.	Next, place around the walls of the room pictures that may represent freedom or the lack of it. Some examples might be: a bird in flight, an American flag, a baby, a Bible, a person running or skiing, a wedding, a woman in the kitchen, a church, an animal in a cage, a wheelchair, and so on.
	Ask each person to choose the picture that best represents freedom to her or him and to go and stand under it. Those who choose the same picture will share why they picked it and why it represents freedom. Then ask each person to choose the picture that least represents freedom and stand under it. Again they should share why they chose the picture.
	Draw out from the group members definitions of freedom. List them on newsprint or chalkboard. *List them all.* There are no wrong answers. Save the definitions until the end of the session.
	B. *Studying the Scriptures* Now that the members of the group have thought about freedom and have tried to define it, it is time to see what the Bible has to say about freedom.

Explanation and Adaptation	Program
	Working alone or in teams, members of the group will look up one of the following passages. It will be helpful if they also read and consider a comment about the verses and discuss the suggested questions, as well as others that the group might develop. Each person or team is then asked to share the main ideas of the passage, what meaning it has for them, and their responses to the questions.
It may be of help to use various translations of each passage. Bibles should be available to use.	**Genesis: 3:1-7, 17-19** The serpent was more crafty than any wild creature that the LORD God had made. He said to the woman, "Is it true that God has forbidden you to eat from any tree in the garden?" The woman answered the serpent, "We may eat the fruit of any tree in the garden, except for the tree in the middle of the garden; God has forbidden us either to eat or to touch the fruit of that; if we do, we shall die." The serpent said, "Of course you will not die. God knows that as soon as you eat it, your eyes will be opened and you will be like gods knowing both good and evil." When the woman saw that the fruit of the tree was good to eat, and that it was pleasing to the eye and tempting to contemplate, she took some and ate it. She also gave her husband some and he ate it. Then the eyes of both of them were opened and they discovered that they were naked; so they stitched fig-leaves together and made themselves loincloths. . . ." And to the man he said: "Because you have listened to your wife and have eaten from the tree which I forbade you, accursed shall be the ground on your account. With labor you shall win your food from it all the days of your life. It will grow thorns and thistles for you, none but wild plants for you to eat. You shall gain your bread by the sweat of your brow until you return to the ground; for from it you were taken. Dust you are, to dust you shall return" (NEB).
If you are working as a total group, the questions might be used to begin the discussion after each passage is read.	"Man is created . . . with the power of exercising freedom of choice. . . . Liberty of choice, however, or free will, is a perilous gift. It may be used either rightly or wrongly, and so there arises the possibility of temptation, of sin, of a 'fall.'" — *The One-Volume Commentary on the Bible* *John R. Dummelow, Editor*
Questions should be written on newsprint or a separate sheet of paper for each small group.	Questions for discussion within the small group: 1. Why do you think God decided to create us as free persons?

Explanation and Adaptation	Program
	2. What are the consequences of the freedom to make choices? 3. Would you rather be free or safe? **John 8:31-36** So Jesus said to those who believed in him, "If you obey my teaching, you are really my disciples; you will know the truth, and the truth will set you free." "We are the descendants of Abraham," they answered, "and we have never been anybody's slaves. What do you mean, then, by saying, 'You will be free'?" Jesus said to them, "I am telling you the truth: everyone who sins is a slave of sin. A slave does not belong to a family permanently, but a son belongs there forever. If the Son sets you free, then you will be really free." (TEV). Discipleship issues in knowledge of the truth. To learn from Jesus is to learn the truth. "You will know the truth," said Jesus. What is that truth? There are many possible answers to that question but the most comprehensive way to put it is that the truth which Jesus brings shows us the real values of life. The fundamental question to which we must consciously or unconsciously give an answer is: "To what am I to give my life? To a career? To the amassing of material possessions? To pleasure? To the service of God?" In the truth of Jesus we see what things are really important and what are not. —William Barclay *The Daily Bible Series* *Gospel of John, Vol. 2* Questions for discussion within the small group: 1. What is the "truth" in Jesus Christ that will really make *you* free? 2. What does it mean to live your life according to that truth? How can you make that truth your own? 3. Can a person in prison or behind the Iron Curtain be really free? **Acts 13:38-39** Let it be known to you therefore, brethren, that through this man forgiveness of sins is proclaimed to you, and by him every one who believes is freed from everything from which you could not be freed by the law of Moses.

Explanation and Adaptation	Program
	Paul knew all too well the futility of rules. . . . Try as he did, he could not keep them all. The harder he tried, the more he broke them. . . . Not until he confronted Christ was he on the right track. To use [an] illustration . . .: The first thing a person who wants to swim has to learn is to trust the water. No matter how perfectly he can make the arm and leg movements, unless he has the confidence to yield himself to the buoyancy of the water and to believe that the water will hold him, all the motions that he can make will be only frantic and futile attempts to do the impossible. . . . It is when a person is able to rest upon and within God that he is then able to improve his own moral and spiritual movements. Before that his activity is little more than panic that proves nothing. In Christ, Paul at last came to rest upon the tender mercy and love of God. . . . The nervous tension and moral strain were at long last relaxed, and he was free to develop every conceivable stroke that would propel him more effectively through the troubled waters of life. —Theodore P. Ferris, Exposition on Acts *The Interpreter's Bible, Vol 9* Questions for discussion within the small group: 1. What is the difference between being free through forgiveness and being free through living by rules? 2. What does it mean to be free from sin? Does it mean that you will never do anything wrong again? 3. How do freedom and permissiveness differ?
If your group would find the first two passages difficult, it may be best to concentrate on the story of the prodigal son. This is particularly true if you have a group of junior high youth.	**Luke 15:11-24** Read this story of the prodigal son. This is a story about one young man's initial folly and his subsequent discovery. His folly was that he thought he could live without a master. His discovery was that there was one master who intended to enrich and bless him. He wanted to be free, free from restraint and restriction . . . but he came to an ignominious end among the pigs. He learned that all freedom is not what it's cracked up to be. The story teaches that commitment to God through Jesus Christ fulfills life rather than restricts it. —LaRue A. Loughhead *Sayings and Doings of Jesus*

Explanation and Adaptation	**Program**
	Questions for discussion within this small group: 1. Have you ever wanted to run away from home? What are the things from which you wanted to be free? 2. Can you say "Jesus is my master"? What changes would you have to make in your life to say that? 3. Is it possible to live entirely free? Would you be happy with absolute freedom?

C. *Discovering the Baptist Tradition*
Prepare on newsprint the following phrases and definitions. Have the group decide which definition best fits a phrase and draw a line connecting the two.

When an individual or group engages in a study of the Scripture as was suggested in the last section of this session, a basic part of Baptist tradition is illustrated. The idea that each person must find the truth and make it her or his own is particularly Baptistic.

The answers are:

    1. — f.
    2. — e.
    3. — b.
    4. — a.
    5. — d.
    6. — c.

1. soul competency	a. The ministry is not limited to the clergy.
2. autonomy of the local church	b. Freedom for all to believe and worship according to their own consciences.
3. religious liberty	c. Each individual has the responsibility to read and interpret God's word in the Bible for himself or herself.
4. priesthood of all believers	d. Religion must be free from state control.
5. separation of church and state	e. Christ has entrusted authority to the entire congregation.
6. individual interpretation of Scripture	f. Every individual has the right to approach God directly.

The heritage and tradition of Baptists, especially American Baptists, are rooted in freedom—freedom of conscience, religious freedom for all, separation of church and state, and the freedom of a local congregation from outside control.

"A part of the Baptist identity has been a strong conviction about the importance of religious liberty. . . .

The heritage for American Baptists is also rooted in the belief that no one should be owned by another person—that the institution of slavery was wrong. Bap-

Explanation and Adaptation	Program

On biblical, theological, historical and rational grounds Baptists took up the cause of religious liberty and in time became the leading champions of it. In fact, this is probably the area in which Baptists have made their greatest contribution to Christianity and the world.

By religious liberty Baptists have meant most basically the freedom to follow their own consciences in determining what they believed, how they defined their mission, how they organized themselves for religious purposes and how they worshipped. Full religious liberty, they maintained, also involves the freedom to express one's beliefs publicly, to recruit new adherents from the larger social order, to organize a religious body free from outside control and to assemble for corporate worship without constraints."

—Eric H. Ohlmann
Statement on Baptist Identity of the Midwest Commission on the Ministry

These stories can be read by the leader to the group.

or

Someone can read a story in advance and be prepared to tell it in his or her own words.

or

Two members of the group could present the story in interview form with one taking the role of the character and the other asking questions to draw out the details of the story.

tists in North America split over the slavery issue, and in 1845 two separate conventions of Baptists were organized, one in the north and one in the south. The Northern Baptist Convention later became the American Baptist Convention and is now the American Baptist Churches. As black Baptist conventions were organized, cooperation developed between these groups and the American Baptist Churches. Today many black churches are members of the ABC and the National Baptist Convention or the Progressive National Baptist Convention.

Out of this tradition came Martin Luther King, Jr., a man who made freedom and equality of rights his life's work and who died in the struggle to achieve those goals. As American Baptists we feel a special kinship with Martin Luther King., Jr., an American Baptist minister. In December 1984, the General Board of the American Baptist Churches passed a resolution calling upon American Baptists to thank God for the life and witness of Dr. King and to participate in Bible study, reflection, and action about the love ethic shown in his writings and actions. The resolution calls upon American Baptists to tell Dr. King's story to their children and grandchildren in order to keep alive the message of his faithful courage and struggles for freedom.

A look at the history of Baptists uncovers the stories of those who believed so strongly in religious liberty and freedom that they were willing to die for what they believed. Here are a few of those stories.

Balthasar Hubmaier: The year was 1524 and I was pastor of the Roman Catholic church in Waldshut, Austria. There was a meeting in my home of delegates from other churches who came with their Bibles to study the Scriptures and to make some revolutionary decisions. Probably because I had an excellent education, I was looked upon as a leader. That got me into much trouble. The meeting became a historic event because we declared independence from the Catholic Church, stating that religion is a voluntary matter, that people are free to interpret the Scriptures for themselves, and that personal faith is the basic tenet. I began to teach and preach about these ideas and soon had to flee because I aroused so much opposition. However, it wasn't long before I was captured and imprisoned. I am very weak from the torture I have endured, and it has

Explanation and Adaptation	**Program**
	just been decreed that I am to be burned at the stake as a heretic. I wonder if anyone will ever remember Balthasar Hubmaier and think of me as a martyr for the freedom I hold dear. **Mary Williams:** I may have been his second choice, but by now my husband admits it was providential that he married me. I was just a maid in the household of the delicate and lovely girl he loved, but when her aristocratic family would not allow her to marry a young man with no prospects, he turned to me. At least I was strong and capable and willing to give him every encouragement. He needed me as we left England to find religious freedom in America. We didn't find it in Massachusetts. When he came to me and said, "Mary, I must flee into the forest tonight," I helped him escape. Roger Williams, my husband, just couldn't stop preaching about religious freedom and "holding aloft the torch of liberty." We paid the price for his beliefs. I took the children and followed him into exile and was at his side when he established, in 1640, the Providence Plantations, a colony which gave the world a new pattern of freedom and liberty of conscience. I also assisted him when he organized the first Baptist church in America. It was a hard life, but it was worth all the suffering and hardships when he secured a charter for the new colony, which we know as Rhode Island, granting liberty in matters of conscience for all people of every race, creed and color. **Obadiah Holmes:** I've had to sleep on my knees and elbows for days and days. Well, I say "sleep," but I have gotten very little rest. I have not been able to lie down because my back and sides have been too raw and painful. You see, I am Obadiah Holmes, a Baptist, arrested in Boston in this year of 1651 for my beliefs about religious freedom. After being imprisoned for more than thirty days, I was stripped and tied to the whipping post. I could have paid a fee and been released, but I felt that would have been too easy. I wanted to show that I really believed in what I had taught and preached. I was given thirty strokes with a three-corded whip. That was equivalent to ninety strokes, and observers said the man wielding the whip spat on his hands and used all his strength. When the whipping ended, the flesh of my back looked like jelly. It is a miracle that I survived. I pray that my suffering for conscience's sake will encourage others to carry on the battle until religious freedom for all is gained.

Explanation and Adaptation	Program
An alternative would be for individuals to write in a journal after the time of reflection.	D. *Making It Personal* Have the group sit quietly for a few minutes and think about the persons from Baptist history who paid a high price for the sake of freedom. Have the following questions listed on newsprint and ask group members to share their responses with one another. 1. Can you think of places in the world today where people are putting their lives on the line for the cause of freedom? 2. Is it easier to struggle and die for political freedom or for religious freedom? 3. Would you be willing and able to suffer for your Baptist beliefs? E. *Closing* Use a fresh sheet of newsprint or clean space on the board and ask participants for definitions of freedom. Compare these with the definitions listed at the beginning of the session. Have their ideas about what freedom is changed during the session?
A part of the worship experience might be a time for youth to make commitments. These could range from a commitment to learn more about Baptist history to a commitment to work for freedom.	The session could close with a time of worship. Choose songs of freedom such as "We Shall Overcome," "Oh, Freedom," or "Lord of the Dance." The Scripture that was used in the portion of the session on "Studying the Scripture" might be read again. End with a prayer of thanksgiving for the tradition and heritage of Christians and of American Baptists and for the religious freedom that we enjoy.

Session **19**

Free to Be Me and Free to Be for Others

Elizabeth J. Loughhead

Explanation and Adaptation	Program

Young people may find it difficult to reconcile the ideas of freedom for themselves and responsibility for the freedom of others.	Objective:
	• To discover what it means to be a free person and to learn that being free also means accepting the responsibility of freedom to others.
	
	Overview of the Session:
	  A. Getting Started
	  B. Experiencing Enslavement
	  C. Dealing with Situations
	  D. Studying the Scriptures
	  E. Making It Personal
	  F. Closing
	
	Resources and Materials Needed:
	  Paper and pencils, newsprint or chalkboard and chalk, Bibles, construction paper, colored markers, scissors, and glue.
	
	The Session in Detail:
	
	A. *Getting Started*
	  Give the members of the group paper and pencil. Have them think of one person they consider to be truly free. Ask, "Who is the freest person you know? Write down the name of that person and list the reasons why you chose her or him. What makes that person really free?"

As the group shares, you might want to capture these descriptions on newsprint.	Then without sharing the names, discuss what makes a person free. There are *no wrong answers.* All are acceptable. After all have had an opportunity to share, continue the discussion by asking the following:
With younger youth there may be	1. How free are you?

Explanation and Adaptation	Program
some hesitation in sharing their own feelings.	2. What choices have you made thus far today? 3. Were you completely free to make those choices? 4. Were you free or not free to come to the meeting of this group?
	B. *Experiencing Enslavement*
An alternative would be to use a film or video that might help youth see examples of confinement today, such as political prisoners.	Jesus assured us that "if the Son makes you free, you will be free indeed" (John 8:36). To "be free indeed" implies that there must be freedom from something. Have the group think of the things that keep them from being free—the things that enslave them.
	Make a list, perhaps including such things as these: school work parental expectations pressure from friends bad habits (drugs, alcohol, smoking) styles of clothing material possessions money worry prejudice rules and laws sex drives
If the group is not able to be serious about the exercise as described, use heavy objects such as large books instead of hands. The pile of objects should be large enough and heavy enough to represent enslavement. If the group is a creative one, ask them to find objects that represent the things on the list. For example: school work—a large notebook possessions—a radio styles—a pair of shoes	When the list is complete, ask one person to sit in a chair or lie on the floor. Other members of the group then choose one thing from the list; as they name it, they place a hand on the person and press down. The person should feel pinned down, trapped, imprisoned. Then the group members slowly remove the pressures one by one by gently removing their hands.
	The person then describes how she or he felt when weighted down and how it felt to be free again.
	C. *Dealing with Situations* The following paragraphs present situations in which a young person is engaged in the struggle to be free. Divide into three small groups and give each group one situation to role-play for the total group. After each role-play, allow time for discussion of possible solutions by the total group. A part of the discussion should focus on how there can be freedom in each situation.
	1. The Wilsons have a rule that the children in the family may not go out on a school night. Joan, the youngest member of the family, has always resented this rule. She finds it restrictive and unrea-

Explanation and Adaptation	Program
	sonable. She feels she should be free to decide whether she should stay home and study or go out for some activity or other.
	It is Tuesday and once again Joan is asking permission to break the rule. She argues that her homework is finished and that she wants to attend a neighborhood Bible study group. Her dad insists that she always wants to break the rule, that her brothers had to live by the house rules, and that she can study the Bible at home or even do some extra school work to bring up her grades.
An alternative would be for the group to create their own role-play situations based on their own experience.	2. Jack has been working extra hours at his job and has found satisfaction in seeing his bank account grow. He is saving to go to college. He will be the first one of his family ever to attend college. He knows that his parents will not be able to help him financially when he is ready to go. He has already talked with the representative of the school of his choice, and he knows how much money he will need. He is positive that by saving every paycheck he can reach his goal. But now his best friend has asked him to go on a camping trip with him and a few other friends. They will share the cost of gas and food. Jack would also lose the pay for the days he would be away. He has said no, but his friend won't take no for an answer. He tells Jack that he isn't any fun anymore and that the guys will cross him off their list if he won't join in.
	3. Gail and Laurie are at the mall on a shopping spree. Both girls have money that was given them at Christmas for new clothes. They head for the store that stocks the latest styles for teenagers and begin to try on garments. Laurie looks adorable in them, but Gail realizes that these styles are not for her. She wants to go to a store where she can buy the items with the tailored look that suits her best.
	Laurie argues that she should buy the fad clothes anyway. She tries to persuade Gail that she needs to dress like the other girls, that the boys won't notice her if she isn't in style, and that it really doesn't matter if she looks good in the clothes or not.
	D. *Studying the Scriptures* As a beginning to the Scripture study, the following can be shared as a minilecture:

Explanation and Adaptation	Program
	The Bible can help persons understand that they can be free. In Christ all are set free. In Galatians 5:1 Paul says, "Freedom is what we have—Christ has set us free!" (TEV). God's gift of freedom, given through God's Son, is undeserved and unearned. It is freely given because God loves humankind so much.
	Many verses of Scripture speak of freedom *from*—from sin, from slavery. Freedom in Christ, however, is not merely freedom *from*, it is freedom *to*. The Declaration of Independence sought freedom from oppression and injustice. Freedom in Christ brings one freedom to become a person living life to the fullest. It enables one to accept God's grace—to find God's forgiveness—to open oneself up to relationships with others, and to grow as a new person in Jesus Christ. Jesus said, "I came that they may have life, and have it abundantly" (John 10:10).
	But, such freedom has its risks. Openness creates vulnerability. To be open to others involves the risk of being touched by their lives, hurt by their hurts, and moved by their concerns. To be open to God involves willingness to face God's demands. To accept God's gift of freedom is to accept the risks of living as free persons, the risks of living life abundantly and the risks of sharing with others. Freedom in Christ is not only a risky business; it also brings responsibility.
Bibles should be available. It is helpful to compare the passages from various translations.	In the Scriptures there is a paradox: *free—yet—not free*. Divide the group into pairs or triads to reflect on the following Scripture and quotes. You will want to have the quotes on newsprint and placed where they can be used by all groups.
	Galatians 5:13 For you were called to freedom, my brothers and sisters, only do not use your freedom as an opportunity for the flesh, but through love be servants of one another *(from An Inclusive Language Lectionary).*
	1 Peter 2:16 Live as free men [persons], yet without using your freedom as a pretext for evil; but live as servants of God.
	Romans 6:17-22 But thanks be to God, that you who were once slaves of sin have become obedient from the heart to the standards of teaching to which you were committed, and, having been set free from sin, have become slaves of

Explanation and Adaptation	Program

righteousness. I am speaking in human terms, because of your natural limitations. For just as you once yielded your members to impurity and to greater and greater iniquity, so now yield your members to righteousness for sanctification. When you were slaves of sin, you were free in regard to righteousness. But then what return did you get from the things of which you are now ashamed? The end of those things is death. But now that you have been set free from sin and have become slaves of God, the return you get is sanctification and its end, eternal life.

"As a great saint put it, the Christian's maxim is, 'Love God and do what you like.' It is the power of that love, and not the constraint of law, that will keep us right; for love is always more powerful than law."
—William Barclay
The Daily Study Bible Series, Galatians

"The Christian cannot abandon self to an earthly, material, godless conduct. A Christian's freedom must be one of service, motivated by love, a freedom for others."
—Joseph A. Fitzmeyer
The Jerome Biblical Commentary

"I set down first these two propositions concerning the liberty and bondage of the spirit: A Christian man is a perfectly free lord of all, subject to none. A Christian man is a perfectly dutiful servant of all, subject to all."
—Martin Luther

Have each small group respond to the following:
1. How can you be free and yet be a servant of God?
2. If you are to be a "slave of righteousness," what does that mean for your life?
3. What is meant by the "constraint of love"? Is that different from the "constraint of law"? Can you give an example?

As a second step, have each small group combine with a second small group and share similarities and differences in their responses. Then as a total group quickly recap the essence of the sharing that has occurred in the two small groups.

E. *Making It Personal*
A person cannot accept God's gift of freedom, according to the Scripture passages just studied, without also accepting the demands of that freedom. Everyone

Explanation and Adaptation	Program
	needs spiritual freedom but needs also to express that freedom in social situations. Responsible love insists that no one is free until all are free. That the bonds of poverty, ignorance, prejudice, injustice, and immorality must be broken is surely the responsibility of the one who would find freedom in Christ. To stand before God as a free person is to stand with all who struggle for freedom.

Have the following situations on newsprint and posted around the room. Ask the group to walk around the room, reading each one and deciding which one they would like to respond to. When all are in a group, share the following statement: "As a free person, I can act as a servant of God in this situation by _____." Each person in the group should reflect on the statement and then share his or her response with the others (in that group). When all within the group have shared, together they should create a way to share their responses. This might be by developing a commercial or talk-show format.

1. Your church is to vote on becoming a "sanctuary" church, a refuge for illegal aliens primarily from El Salvador. You know that several people have already been arrested because they helped harbor Salvadorans. You have been told that representatives of the Immigration and Naturalization Service will be present at the church meeting. You had planned to attend.

2. You live down the street from a young man who was badly injured in an accident. He is paralyzed from the waist down and is confined to a wheelchair. His boss has offered him his former job back, but in order to accept he must find a way to get across town. The medical expenses have caused his family to sell their car, and they cannot afford to buy another. The young man's monthly disability checks barely cover living expenses. The local transportation service does not have a bus equipped to handle a wheelchair.

3. Your parents have just inherited quite a large sum of money from a distant relative who died. For the first time they have the funds to establish an investment portfolio. After talking with a financial counselor they bring home the list of companies in which it has been recommended that they buy stock. You

Explanation and Adaptation	Program
	realize that three of these companies operate in South Africa and cooperate with the government of that country in maintaining apartheid, the restrictive and often brutal policy against the black citizens of that nation.
	4. Your next-door neighbor is eighty-one years old. She is still able to care for herself and can live alone. You notice that you haven't seen her lately and decide to go over and call on her. After you ring the bell you become aware that she has peeked from behind the curtains a couple of times to check on who you are. When she finally comes to the door it takes a long time before you can go in because she must unlock two locks, release a chain and unfasten the storm door. Inside as you chat with her you notice that the newspaper on the table has articles about robberies and muggings circled in black ink.
	F. *Closing* Suggest that the members of the group look at the paper on which they wrote the name of the freest person they know and the reasons why they chose that person. Would they still choose that person as "the most free"? Have their ideas about freedom and being a free person changed?
	Let the group plan a closing worship moment. This should be creative worship and should grow out of the experiences the group has had together as they have studied about freedom.
	The leader might suggest: • writing new words to a familiar hymn tune, using thoughts about freedom; • paraphrasing a Scripture passage about freedom, putting it in words the group uses in everyday life; • creating a prayer and expressing it through motion or dance; • drawing a picture or making a poster to illustrate enslavement and freedom; • symbolically offering to God the things that enslave them and showing by body language that they are now free.
If symbolic objects were used in the exercise on experiencing enslavement, these could be offered.	End with a time of quiet reflection.
	The following litany and prayer could be used if time will not permit the group to create their own worship.

Explanation and Adaptation	Program
	Litany of Freedom

Leader: O God, you created us and gave us the gift of freedom.

Response: We thank you for freedom.

Leader: We know that freedom brings the responsibility of making choices.

Response: Help us to choose the right.

Leader: In our freedom we have sometimes lost the vision of liberty and justice for all.

Response: Forgive us, O God.

Leader: We have sometimes oppressed those weaker than we are.

Response: Forgive us, O God.

Leader: We have taken pride in the heritage of justice in our land yet have not always treated others justly.

Response: Forgive us, O God.

Leader: We have been proud of our freedom yet have not spoken out against tyranny where it exists in the world.

Response: Forgive us, O God.

Leader: For the gift of freedom and for the promise of your presence and power as we seek to live as free persons,

Response: We praise you and thank you, O God.

Prayer: We need your forgiveness, O God. Forgive us when we have been indifferent toward those who are hungry, homeless, jobless, and lonely in our world. Forgive us when we have not spoken strongly and clearly for economic justice for the oppressed—Indians, Hispanics, blacks, women, all minorities. Renew us, we pray, to a fresh commitment to freedom for all. Where there is oppression, help us to bring liberation. Free us from the slavery to our own selfishness and greed that all the people of the world may share resources of food and fuel. Reassure us of your continuing love so that we may be liberated in joyful thanksgiving to care for others who need our help and our love. Amen.

Mercy
Clara E. Wong

Explanation and Adaptation	Program
	Objectives: • To help participants gain a richer meaning of the word "mercy." • To help participants translate that meaning into their daily relationships and commitments. Overview of the Session: A. Relationships and Belonging: Freedom and Commitment B. Mercy Seen as Faithfulness and Loyalty C. Hard Examples D. What Will Mercy Mean for Us? E. Conclusion Resources and Materials Needed: Bibles in various translations, newsprint, markers, magazines, newspapers. The Session in Detail:
Bring in some short legal documents to give participants a flavor of the wording of such instruments. Your local library will probably have sample documents. Some issues to consider might be how to share work, how income should be distributed, who will be responsible for child care, and so on.	A. *Relationships and Belonging: Freedom and Commitment* Divide the group into smaller working groups. Ask them to design a marriage contract in the form of a legal document to cover all aspects of this relationship. Tell them it is to be a contract that two people planning to marry would have to sign before getting married. Suggest some situations that might arise in a marriage relationship as a way to start them thinking. Bring the groups back to share their contracts. Change, add to, or subtract from the conditions listed. Now ask them to go back to their teams again and write a statement of relationship for best friends. This

Explanation and Adaptation	Program
	simple statement will cover all aspects of their relationship. Bring the groups back to share these statements. What, if any, differences are expressed in the conditions listed?
Note these on newsprint if helpful.	Ask participants to discuss the pros and cons of each document.
Put on newsprint these points about the word *hesed*.	B. *Mercy Seen as Faithfulness and Loyalty* Pair up or group individuals to examine several Scripture passages. Tell them that the word *hesed* has been translated "mercy," "loyalty," and "faithfulness." *Hesed* is a Hebrew word rich in meaning. 1 Samuel 20 2 Samuel 16:15–17:16 Joshua 2 Genesis 12
An alternative would be to do this as a whole group, taking each Scripture and discussing it as a total group. You may find it helpful to have the questions listed on newsprint.	Ask them to respond to these questions: • What are the conditions that created the need for mercy or loyalty or faithfulness? • What kind of a relationship is mentioned? • Is there a sense of freedom to do something or a necessity to act? • What would happen if mercy was not given? • What would have happened to the person who refused loyalty from the person who is requesting faithfulness?
Prepare in advance on newsprint. An alternative is to make notes on these points and if they do not come out as a result of the group discussion, include them in your summary of this section.	**1 Samuel 20:** The issue of loyalty comes within an existing relationship. It is an act that strengthens a relationship but is not something that first brings the relationship into being. It means honoring relationships even in drastic changes of circumstance.
	2 Samuel 16:15–17:16: Loyalty is a quality to be given in a situation of urgent need. The exercise of loyalty brings risk and the need for hard choices. Obligation and freedom of choice are joined together.
	Joshua 2: The right choice is not easy to discern. Choices are difficult. The one asking for mercy is in a dependent role with no recourse if the other decides not to respond to the need.

Explanation and Adaptation	Program
	Genesis 12: Loyalty asks us to do what is right for a relationship even though opportunity to do otherwise is offered.
If step B was done as a total group, you might want to work in pairs first and have each pair respond to these examples. Then as a total group they could share their findings and discuss what they see as the implications of what they suggest. *Note:* Be sensitive to the feelings of persons in your group. For some youth these may not be theoretical examples but situations within their own experience.	C. *Hard Examples* In an open discussion, take time to consider the hard choices being given in the following situations: • A relative is too sick to take care of herself or himself. Should this person be sent to a nursing home or should this person live in the family household? What needs will be met or not met for other family members? • If a child were to commit a misdemeanor, should the parents show loyalty and mercy to the child by covering up what happened or should they report it to the authorities? • Marriages do not always mature well. When should a divorce be considered and when should partners try to start over again in forgiveness? • If we always are going to have people hungry in this world, are we obligated to try to feed everyone? • If every person is a precious gift of life, are we to keep someone alive at all costs? If not, why?
Prepare these statements in advance on newsprint.	D. *What Will Mercy Mean for Us?* 1. Our lifestyle of faithfulness is grounded in God's faithfulness to us. Our faithful God overcomes our failure to be faithful to each other; in forgiveness we can try again. 2. There are no easy answers for tough situations; there is no correct answer that fits all situations. There are no absolutes. 3. We must not let uncertainty paralyze us into inaction.
As the group works on the mural, encourage them to think of a variety of situations, such as the illustrations in "Hard Examples" or situations from their own experience.	What are some situations facing us, this nation, and the world that ask us to be merciful? Have the group members, using magazines and newspapers, create a mural of situations that call us to be merciful. They might use headlines and/or pictures that speak of needs in your community, the nation, and the world at large. If time permits, the group might also develop a second mural that shows ways to respond to need, ways in which mercy can be shown.
	E. *Conclusion* Loyalty calls us to take all relationships seriously. Faithfulness calls us to examine our priorities and to choose a way of life in which we show mercy to all.

Explanation and Adaptation	Program
If as a leader you would like to read more on this subject, the excellent resource used by the author is *Faithfulness in Action: Loyalty in Biblical Perspective*, by Katharine Doob Sakenfeld (Philadelphia: Fortress Press, 1985).	After a few minutes of silent reflection, ask the group to share prayer concerns. These may be for situations in need of mercy or they may be more personal concerns—for commitment, help to be stronger, and so on. Persons should not feel pressured to share. After all who wish to have had a time to share, have the prayer.